THE INTERNATIONAL
PSYCHO-ANALYTICAL
LIBRARY

No. 107

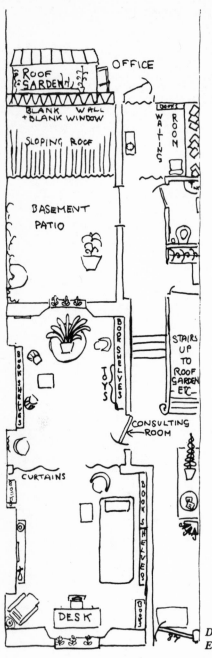

PLAN OF
DR. WINNICOTT'S
WORKING SPACE
AT
87 CHESTER SQUARE
LONDON

Drawn by
E. Britton

THE INTERNATIONAL PSYCHO-ANALYTICAL LIBRARY
EDITED BY M. MASUD R. KHAN
No. 107

THE PIGGLE

*An Account of the Psychoanalytic
Treatment of a Little Girl*

by

D. W. WINNICOTT

Edited by

Ishak Ramzy

LONDON
THE HOGARTH PRESS
AND THE INSTITUTE OF PSYCHO-ANALYSIS
1978

PUBLISHED BY
THE HOGARTH PRESS LTD
40 WILLIAM IV STREET
LONDON WC2N 4DG

British Library Cataloguing
in Publication Data

Winnicott, Donald Woods
    The piggle. — (The international psycho-
analytical library; no. 107).
    1. Child analysis — Cases, clinical reports,
statistics
    I. Title II. Ramzy, Ishak III. Series
    618.928'9170926   RJ504.2

    ISBN 0-7012-0451-6

Printed and bound in Great Britain by
Redwood Burn Ltd.
Trowbridge and Esher

Contents

PREFACE

This book presents verbatim excerpts from a psychoanalyst's notes on the treatment of a young child. The reader has the rare opportunity of being admitted to the intimacy of the consulting room and of studying the child and the therapist at work. While it will be of special value to those professionally involved with children, it will also be of interest to anyone concerned with children and their development.

The Piggle will be of particular interest to those familiar with the writings of the late Dr. Winnicott. His comments and other occasional notes for the reader describe the treatment as it develops, and give his theoretical understanding of what is happening. At the same time the text of what he said, and how he said it, illustrates vividly his contributions to psychoanalytic theory and technique in the treatment of children. But this is not a heavy textbook. It is a lively account of two people working and playing together with purposeful intensity and enjoyment. In Winnicott's view "it is not possible for a child of this age to get meaning out of a game unless first of all the game is *played* and *enjoyed.*" It is through enjoyment that anxiety is mastered and contained within the total experience (Consultation 13).

Readers will sense Winnicott's own enjoyment in his play with the child. He perceives and accepts the transference, but he does much more; he brings it to life by enacting the various roles allotted to him. The dramatization of the child's inner world enables her to experience and play with those fantasies which most disturb her. This occurs in small doses and in a setting which has become safe enough through the skill of the therapist. The creative tension in the transference is maintained, and the level of anxiety and suspense is kept within the child's capacity, so that playing can continue.

Dr. Winnicott adapted his technique to the needs of each particular case. If full psychoanalysis was needed and was possible, he would do analysis. Otherwise, he varied his technique from regular sessions to sessions "on demand," or to single or extended therapeutic consultations. In this case the "on demand" method was used.

In the manuscript of this book, Dr. Winnicott had left a memo to remind himself to make a comment on his way of working with the parents of the patient. Unfortunately, he never wrote this out in full, but his cryptic notes indicate something of what he felt about his working relationship with them. His notes read as follows: "Share material with the parents—not family therapy—not casework—psychoanalysis *partagé* (shared). No breach of confidence on their part, and they didn't interfere."

There is also a note suggesting that both the sharing with the parents and the spacing of the interviews had the effect of diluting possessiveness, leaving the way open for the patient's relationship to her parents to develop as part of the total therapeutic process. Readers will appreciate that in the case of the Piggle, the parents were professional people who had knowledge of the psychotherapeutic field. Their collaboration was crucial to the outcome of the work.

The therapy extended over two and a half years, with infrequent meetings. During the intervals the patient often sent messages and drawings in her parents' letters to tell Dr. Winnicott how she was feeling. It was vital to the therapeutic task that meetings were arranged at the child's request, and this technique was of paramount importance in maintaining the relationship. The strength of the transference held throughout and was resolved finally in a moving and convincing way to the satisfaction of both.

Clare Winnicott

R.D. Shepherd
Winnicott Publications Committee

EDITOR'S FOREWORD

To introduce this book by the late Dr. Donald W. Winnicott is a privilege and an honor. He had written this intimate and fascinating clinical document and set it aside for several years before he decided to present it to any readers other than Mrs. Clare Winnicott and the parents of the little patient he had cared for. I came to know of the manuscript by a chance that only a Winnicott could arrange, a year and a half before his death in 1971. The notes of my extended discussions with him during the summer of 1969 and our subsequent correspondence designed to be of assistance to him in preparing the book for publication have been the guidelines I followed to edit it on his behalf. Much of what he only could have done and planned to do if he had the time to revise certain passages and expand several brief notes will be left undone in order to keep this contribution within the format and the style that Winnicott had originally set for it. As it stands, however, it is likely destined to remain an eloquent example of rare clinical acumen and an invaluable illustration of the theory and technique of one of the most creative and outstanding masters of psychoanalytic treatment at work with a child.

A few facts about Winnicott may need to be mentioned, especially to those readers who may have had no access to a biographical account of him. Born to truly English parents and raised in comfortable circumstances, Winnicott qualified in medicine in his early twenties. He started his career as a pediatrician serving as physician to Paddington Green Children's Hospital in London for about forty years, during which he estimated he had seen some 60,000 mothers and children. Shortly after he started to practice pediatrics, he contacted Ernest Jones who referred him for analysis with James Strachey. About those years, Winnicott writes, "I was starting up as consultant pediatrician at that time, and you can imagine how exciting it was to be taking innumerable case histories and to be getting from uninstructed hospital-class parents all the confirmation that anyone could need for the psychoanalytic theories that were beginning to have meaning for me through my own analysis. At that time no other analyst was also a pediatrician, and so for two or three decades I was an isolated phenomenon." [1]

Fame and world reputation came to him during the last fifteen years of his life. He had not established a school; neither had he led a group of followers who spread his teachings. He gained recognition through the unassuming but direct manner and the simple but inimitable style in which he presented his findings. In spoken or written words, he presented vivid examples of his actual work — convincing evidence for his findings — to the scientific circles and journals of specialists in psychiatry and psychoanalysis, and more often to the much wider circles of parents, social workers, teachers, and all those concerned with education, mental health, and child care services. Winnicott made history in the science of human nature for discovering the significance of what people

1 A Personal View of the Kleinian Contribution. In: *The Maturational Processes and the Facilitating Environment.* New York: International Universities Press; London: Hogarth Press, 1965, p. 172.

had known all along without realizing it or estimating its importance for human growth and fulfillment. A bibliography, not updated, of his published books and papers runs into 190 titles.[2] To sum up even the main themes of such a voluminous contribution would itself fill a whole book, but an exposition of the essence of Winnicott's contributions can be gleaned from Masud Khan's introduction to the new edition of Winnicott's collected papers, *Through Paediatrics to Psycho-Analysis.*[3]

Having been one of my most esteemed teachers, Donald Winnicott, for almost twenty years, was to me friend and consultant. As it was my custom to pass through London whenever I went to the International Psycho-Analytical Congress in Europe, I wrote Winnicott in June 1969 wondering if he would have the time for a visit and a conversation before we both got busy with the pre-Congress activities on the way to Rome. He promptly answered me suggesting an evening soon after my arrival in London. But in a later mail, the same day, I received another letter which said:

"I have some news for you. You don't know it, but on 22nd July 2:30 - 4:15 p.m. you are going to supervise *me* in front of all the pre-Congress visitors!

"The thing is, because of my illness some of my students had to go elsewhere for supervision and I haven't got a student with a very good case for me to supervise just about then. So I have asked permission to be supervised in the passive voice and I am asking you to do this.

"I shall give a child analysis hour, and you may find it pretty awful as analysis, but this should lead to discussion. I look forward to this experience with zest. When we meet I can

2 See Editor's List in *The Maturational Processes and the Facilitating Environment.*
3 London: Hogarth Press, 1975.

let you know anything more you want to know, if this is necessary. I do hope you just simply will do this."

Soon after my arrival in London, one evening after a
sumptuous dinner Clare had prepared for us, Winnicott told
me about the function we were scheduled for on July 22 as part
of the pre-Congress Scientific Program offered by the British
Psycho-Analytic Society. When I inquired if there were any
notes I could read to acquaint myself with the case, he half-
seriously said that I need not spend any time on preparation,
nor did I need to clutter my mind with any details other than
those he was going to present and upon which I could base my
supervisory remarks and lead an open discussion at the meeting. It was only after a playful exchange that he handed me a
whole copy of the typewritten notes of the case out of which he
had not yet decided which portion he would present.

Upon my return to the hotel, out of my concern over the
audience's disappointment in not seeing Winnicott doing
supervision, as had been announced, in order to see him
supervised instead, and by a less known colleague at that, I
hurriedly flipped through the pages of the manuscript to learn
something about its contents and to see how the presentation
discussion could go. As if I had stumbled on a trove of art, my
thrill and delight with what I read dispelled my concern and
made me look forward to the function with joyous anticipation. This book now presents that manuscript to the reader.

The seats of the large amphitheater were all occupied,
and latecomers had to be content with standing room only.
From the available list of registrants for the meeting, the
audience included psychoanalysts from the four corners of the
world, with only a few from Britain, since the pre-Congress
Scientific Program was offered mainly for the visitors from
overseas. After explaining why he was not going to demon-
strate a supervision of his but be supervised by me instead, at

his own invitation, Winnicott in his soft voice and unassuming manner proceeded to introduce the case and to present the work he had done during the first session with the patient. One issue in the subsequent discussion centered on the subject of whether the type of treatment Winnicott described and called "psychoanalysis on demand" with its infrequent and irregular sessions was analysis or psychotherapy. Winnicott replied by directing attention to what he did with the transference and the unconscious, not to the formal arrangements of the analytic situation, or the frequency or regularity of the analytic sessions. In the course of this discussion an impatient listener was heard to say in an audible whisper: "If there is any question that this is an analysis, how is it that the case of Little Hans[4] is still considered one of the classics in psychoanalytic literature?" In his own introduction to this book Winnicott discusses the advantages of the "on demand" method.

The fact is that Winnicott had already defined his view of what a psychoanalysis is in 1958[5] when he said: "I have been invited to refer to *psychoanalytic treatment,* and to balance this a colleague has been invited to refer to *individual psychotherapy.* I expect we both start off with the same problem: how to distinguish between the two? Personally I am not able to make this distinction. For me the question is: has the therapist had an analytic training or not?

"Instead of contrasting our two subjects each with the other, we might more profitably contrast our two subjects with that of child psychiatry. In my practice I have treated thou-

4 Freud, S. (1909), Analysis of a Phobia in a Five-Year-Old Boy. *Standard Edition,* 10:3-149. London: Hogarth Press, 1955.
5 Child Analysis in the Latency Period. In: *The Maturational Processes and the Facilitating Environment.* New York: International Universities Press, 1965; London: Hogarth Press, p. 115.

sands of children in this age group [latency] by child psy-chiatry. I have (as a trained analyst) given individual psycho-therapy to some hundreds. Also I have had a certain number of children of this age group for psychoanalysis, more than twelve and less than twenty. The borders are so vague that I would be unable to be exact."

A few years later (1962),[6] he came back to the subject and said: "I enjoy myself doing analysis and I always look forward to the end of each analysis. Analysis for analysis' sake has no meaning for me. I do analysis because that is what the patient needs to have done and to have done with. If the patient does not need analysis, then I do something else. In analysis one asks: how *much* can one be allowed to do? And, by contrast, in my clinic the motto is: how *little* need be done?"

He concludes the same paper with the following state-ment: "In my opinion our aims in the practice of the standard technique are not altered if it happens that we interpret mental mechanisms which belong to the psychotic types of disorder and to primitive stages in the emotional stages of the individual. If our aim continues to be to verbalize the nascent conscious in terms of the transference, then we are practising analysis; if not, then we are analysts practising something else that we deem to be appropriate to the occasion. And why not?"

Ishak Ramzy, M.A., Ph.D.
Topeka, Kansas, October, 1974

6 The Aims of Psycho-Analytical Treatment. In: *The Maturational Processes and the Facilitating Environment*. New York: International Univer-sities Press; London: Hogarth Press, 1965, pp. 166-70.

INTRODUCTION

This book, which is offered under my name, is partly written by the parents of a little girl nicknamed the Piggle.[1] The book is composed of excerpts from letters written jointly about Gabrielle and of my clinical notes attempting to give a detailed description of the psychoanalytic interviews. I have added comments, but not enough—it is hoped—to prevent the reader from developing a personal view of the material and its evolution.

The question arises whether it is fair or unfair to publish intimate details of any analysis, but the fact that in this case the patient was only two years, four months old when the treatment started makes the decision easier. Also, by taking partial responsibility, the parents have shown that they consider this published description of the treatment will not do harm to Gabrielle if she comes across the book when she is older.[2]

I would not describe this treatment as finished. It is doubtful to me whether a child analysis ought to be thought of

[1] In England the nickname "Piggle" is a term of endearment often used with young children.

[2] At a later date the mother offered a few comments on the transcript of the sessions with no view to publication. Some of these have come to be included in the book.

as complete when the patient is so young that the developmental processes simply take over as the analysis begins to succeed. It can be seen in this case that at first the child's illness dominates the scene, so that it is easy to ascribe clinical improvement to work done in analysis. In time, however, the child begins to get free from the pattern of rigid defense organization that constitutes the illness, and then it becomes very difficult to distinguish between clinical improvement and emotional development, between work done in the treatment and the maturational processes that have now become freed.

The parents made contact with me in January 1964 when Gabrielle was two years, four months. I saw Gabrielle 14 times "on demand" starting when she was two years, five months. She was five years old at the time of the 14th session.

In this particular analysis, because of the fact that the child lived a considerable distance from London, the treatment was done "on demand," and this affects the question of the ending of the treatment. There is no reason why the "on demand" method should not be continued and perhaps from time to time include phases of intensive treatment. The distant future cannot be and need not be predicted. It will be observed, however, in this connection, that the analyst is liable to be more tolerant of the child's symptomatology than the parents who tend, once a child has come into treatment, to feel that the appearance of symptoms must always mean a return of the child to treatment. Once a child has started treatment what is lost sight of is the rich symptomatology of all children who are being cared for in their own satisfactory homes. It is possible for the treatment of a child actually to interfere with a very valuable thing which is the ability of the child's home to tolerate and to cope with the child's clinical states that indicate emotional strain and temporary holdups in emotional development, or even the fact of development itself.

In this respect the "on demand" method has advantages over the method of the daily session five times a week. On the other hand, it should not be thought that a compromise is valuable; either the child should have analysis on the basis of a daily session or else should be seen on demand. The once-a-week treatments that have become almost an accepted compromise are of doubtful value, falling between the two stools and preventing really deep work from being done.

The reader may find that the clinical state of this child is well described in the letters the parents wrote between the treatment hours. It is possible to see from these descriptions, which were written without any idea of publication and simply to inform the analyst, that Gabrielle's illness became more of a dominating feature and clearly organized as an illness pattern after the first couple of sessions. Then, gradually, the illness pattern dissolved to some extent, giving way to a series of maturational stages that had to be worked over again although they had certainly been experienced satisfactorily in Gabrielle's infancy, i.e., before the mother's pregnancy. It is from the description of the psychoanalytic work, however, that the reader can see the essential health in this child's personality, a quality that was always evident to the analyst even when clinically and at home the child was really ill. The treatment had a momentum of its own that was evident from its inception, and no doubt enhanced by the parents' and the patient's confidence in the analyst. The descriptions of the work done show that, from the beginning, Gabrielle came to do work, and that each time when she came for treatment she brought a problem she was able to display. On each occasion the analyst had a sense of being informed by the child of a specific problem, although there were many areas of indeterminate play or behavior or conversation in which there seemed to be no orientation. These phases of indeterminate play were evidently an important feature in that out of the chaos a sense of direction developed and the child became able to communicate out of a sense of real need, a need that had prompted her to ask for another session. I have purposely left the vague material vague, as it was for me at the time when I was taking notes.

D. W. Winnicott, F.R.C.P.

November 22, 1965

THE PATIENT

EXTRACT FROM INITIAL LETTER FROM THE
PARENTS, WRITTEN BY THE MOTHER
JANUARY 4, 1964

"Can you spare time to see our daughter Gabrielle who is two years, four months old? She has worries, and they keep her awake at night, and sometimes they seem to affect the general quality of her life and of her relationship with us, though not always.

"Here are a few details.

"It is difficult to describe her as a baby; she seemed very much a person, giving one the feeling of great inner resources. There is little to report about the feeding; it seemed to happen easily and naturally; so did weaning. *She was breast-fed for nine months.*[1] She had great poise — hardly ever fell, when she learned to walk, and hardly ever cried when she fell. From the earliest times she showed very passionate

---

[1] My italics. D.W.W.

5

feelings toward her father, and was somewhat high-handed with her mother.

"She had a little sister (now seven months) when she was twenty-one months old, which I considered far too early for her. And both this and (I would think also) our anxiety about it[2] seemed to bring about a great change in her.

"She becomes easily bored and depressed which was not evident before, and is suddenly very conscious of her relationships and especially of her identity. The acute distress, and the overt jealousy of her sister, did not last long, though the distress was very acute. These two now find one another very amusing. Toward her mother, whose existence she had almost appeared to ignore, Gabrielle shows much more warmth, though sometimes also more resentment. She has become very obviously reserved toward her father.

The illness clinically described

"I shall not try to give you any more details of this, but just tell you about the fantasies that keep her calling to us till late at night.

"She has a black mummy and daddy. The black mummy comes in after her at night and says: "Where are my yams?" (To yam = to eat. She pointed out her breasts, calling them yams, and pulling them to make them larger.) Sometimes she is put into the toilet by the black mummy. The black mummy, who lives in her tummy, and who can be talked to there on the tele-

[2] I did not know until much later that the mother herself had experienced the birth of a sibling at this very age. D.W.W.

phone, is often ill, and difficult to make better.

"The second strand of fantasy, which started earlier, is about the 'babacar.' Every night she calls, again and again: 'Tell me about the babacar, *all* about the babacar.' The black mummy and daddy are often in the babacar together, or some man alone. There is very occasionally a black Piggle in evidence (we call Gabrielle 'the Piggle').

"There was a time, only just past, when she badly scratched her face every night.

"Often she seems vivid and spontaneous and fully alive, but we thought we would ask for your help at this time, lest she should settle down and harden herself against her distress as the only way of coping with it."

EXTRACT FROM LETTER FROM MOTHER

"Things have not by any means improved since I wrote to you. The Piggle hardly ever plays with any concentration now, she hardly even admits to being herself, she is either the baba, or more often the mummy. 'The Piga gone away, gone to the babacar. The Piga is black. Both Pigas are bad. Mummy, cry about the babacar!'

"I told her I had written to Dr. Winnicott 'who understands about babacars and black mummys'; since then she has ceased her nightly pleading: 'Tell me about the babacar.' Twice she asked me, as if out of the blue: 'Mummy take me to Dr. Winnicott.' "

A degenerating clinical state

FIRST CONSULTATION
(February 3, 1964)

The parents brought in "the Piggle" and first we all had some time together in the consulting room. Gabrielle looked serious and it was evident to me that she had come for work as soon as she put her head in the door.

I took all three to the waiting room and then tried to get the Piggle back into my room. She was not quite willing to make this journey, and in the course of going along the passage she said to her mother:

"I'm too shy!"

I therefore got the mother in with her and told her not to help at all, and she sat back on the couch with the Piggle beside her. Already I had made friends with the teddy-bear who was sitting on the floor by the desk. Now I was in the back part of the room, sitting on the floor playing with the toys. I said to the Piggle (whom I could not actually see): "Bring teddy over here, I want to show him the toys." She went immediately and brought the teddy over and

9

helped me to show him the toys. She then
started playing with them herself, mostly taking
parts of trains out of the muddle. She kept on
saying: "I got a ...[whatever it was]." After
about five minutes the mother slipped out into
the waiting room. We left the door open; this
was important for the Piggle, who tested the
arrangements. Then began something which
was repeated over and over again: "Here's
another one ... and here's *another* one." This
had to do mostly with trucks and engines, but it
did not seem to matter much what it was that
she made this comment about. I took this therefore as a communication and said: "Another
baby. The *Sush Baby*."[1] This was evidently the
correct thing to say, because now she started
giving me an account of the time the Sush Baby
came, as she remembered it. What she said was:
"I was a baby. I was in a cot. I was asleep. I just
had the bottle." Then there was something
about licking, as I thought, and I said: "Did you
say you were licking?" And she said: "No, I
wasn't." (In fact, as I found later, she had never
had the bottle, but she had seen the baby on the
bottle.) So then I repeated: "And then there was
another baby" — helping her on with the story of
the birth.

Then she took a round object with a center-
piece that at one time belonged to the axle of a
carriage and said: "Where did this come from?"
I answered realistically, and then I said: "And

*Establishing
communication*

[1] This is what Gabrielle calls her baby sister Susan, now eight months old.

where did the baby come from?" She replied: "De cot." At this point, she took a little man figure and tried to push it into the driver's seat of a toy car. It wouldn't go in because it was too big; she tried putting it through the window and tried every way.

"It won't go in; it's stuck." Then she took a little stick and pushed it in the window and said: "Stick goes in." I said something about man putting something into woman to make baby. She said: "I've got a cat. Next time I'll bring the pussycat, another day."

Anxiety— change of subject

At this point she wanted to see her mother, and she opened the door. I said something about talking to teddy. There was some anxiety that had to be dealt with. I tried to verbalize this: "You feel frightened; do you have frightening dreams?" She said: "About the babacar." This is the name the mother had already given me in connection with the baby, the Sush Baby.

Contact with mother— relief

By this time, Gabrielle was taking the ribbon off the toy lamb and putting it round her own neck. I seem to have said: "What does the babacar eat?" She answered: "I don't know. I got a blue . . . oh no, this was a balloon." (She had brought a deflated balloon with her, and indeed the play had started with a futile manipulation of this thing which she now referred to.)

She now took up a little electric lightbulb with a mat surface and on which there had been drawn the face of a man. She said: "Draw little man." I drew again a man's face on the bulb.

She took the little plastic strawberry baskets and said: "May I put these in?" Then she started packing everything into boxes in a very deliberate way. There were a lot of small oddments around, and about eight boxes of one kind or another. I said to her about this: "You are making babies like cooking, collecting everything together." She made remarks such as: "I must tidy up. Mustn't leave the place untidy."

Eventually, absolutely everything to the minutest detail was packed away into the six boxes. I was wondering how to do what I had to do, and I rather obviously brought in something about the black mummy: "Do you ever feel angry with mummy?" I linked up the idea of a black mummy with her rivalry with her mother because both of them love the same man, daddy. It was very obvious that she was deeply attached to her father, and I felt quite safe in making this interpretation. At one level this must be true.

Denial of muddle

After she had put everything away she said: "I'd like to fetch daddy and mummy." As she went to the waiting room she said: "I've tidied up."

In the course of all this, Gabrielle had co-operated with me in putting away all the toys under the shelf including her own teddy, and we tied the bow once more round the lamb's neck.

I then saw the mother while the father looked after the Piggle in the waiting room.

The mother said that there had been a great change toward ill health in the Piggle recently. She was not naughty and she was nice to the baby. It was difficult to put into words what the matter was. But *she was not herself.* In fact she refused to be herself and said so: "I'm the mummy. I'm the baby." She was not to be addressed as herself. She had developed a high-voiced chatter which was not hers. If she talked seriously, her voice was much deeper. As a baby, the Piggle was unusually self-contained and sure of touch. When Susan was born, the mother was aware immediately that the Piggle needed much more attention. There was a song[2] that was associated with the Piggle's babyhood, but when the parents sang this recently she cried bitterly and said: "Stop. Don't sing this song." (With me, she had hummed a tune and was very pleased when I said: "Ships that come sailing by." I learned this was a song that had been taught her by her father.)

The song she didn't like was a German song with made-up English words and was evidently closely related to the mother's intimate relationship with her baby. The mother's original language was German; the father is English.

[2] Parents' note: "We made an old tune into a lullaby with the refrain: '. . . and the mummy and the daddy will be here. . . .' (i.e., while the baby sleeps). For a long time she had tears in her eyes when someone hummed the tune. We have now given it new words (the original is a parting song); sometimes she likes it now, sometimes she calls: 'Stop!' when someone sings it."

With regard to the black mummy and the babacar, there are details here which I did not clearly understand. The Piggle's nightmares may be about a babacar, also about a train.

This child was not toilet-trained, but when the new baby came she trained herself in a week. She was one of those children who did not speak and then suddenly spoke freely. She used to play all the time, but since the change occurred she tended to lie in her cot and suck her thumb without playing. Her balance had been excellent always, but since the change in her she had been falling and crying and feeling hurt. She used to be high-handed. Her mother was simply someone to be ordered round. From the age of six months, she adored her father, and at that age said: "Daddy!" But she soon forgot or ceased to be able to use the word. Since the change, she seemed to see mother as a separate person and had become affectionate with her and at the same time more reserved toward her father.

Several days later, in a telephone conversation with the mother, I learned that after the consultation the Piggle allowed herself, for the first time since the birth of the sister, to be a baby instead of constantly making a protest. In fact, she went into the carrycot and had innumerable bottles. She was not allowing anybody to call her Piggle, however. She was either the baby or the mother. The Piggles were bad and black. "I am the baby." The mother seemed to feel that Gabrielle was not distressed enough. She had a way of symbolizing her experiences, as the mother put it. Both parents felt helpless. They did not seem to be able to see the positive aspects of the child's ability to solve things by internal processes. On the other hand, they were right in not being satisfied with the present condition.

The Piggle lay in bed and cried without knowing why. As they left me, she said: "The babacar," as if she had forgotten something. She then said: "Dr. Winnicott doesn't know about babacars—about the babacar." She also said that teddy wanted to go back to London and play with Dr. Winnicott, but she didn't want to. Incidentally, she had nearly left the teddy among the toys, but at the last minute remembered him and took him home with her. It is as if she were regretting all the time not being able to tell Dr. Winnicott about the babacar. The parents were reminded of the earlier agony of tension that she had about the black mummy and the babacar until "something snapped," as it were. The mother did not know the exact origin of the babacar, but it was linked with black, black mummy, black self, and black people. In the middle of nice happenings, Gabrielle suddenly looked worried and said: "The babacar" and this spoiled everything. This is consistent with the idea that black here meant that hate had come in (or disillusionment).

Belief in the analyst

Disillusionment

There is one other detail, which is that sometimes mother must fall and hurt herself,

and then the Piggle makes the mother better.
Here again is more evidence, if it is needed, of
the hate and love of the mother appearing
simultaneously, and of the Piggle's ability to
use the mother aggressively. To this one must be
able to add the question: falling is becoming
pregnant. In this way, the father's aggression is
included.

Ambivalence

COMMENTS

I felt that the interview and the report
from the mother justified my having taken the
word "shy" as the key word. The patient was in
process of working out a new relationship to the
mother which took into account her hate of her
mother because of her love of her father. The
six-months'-old love of her father was not assim-
ilated in her total personality and lay alongside
a relationship to the mother who, at that time,
was still a subjective object.[3]

The change related to the birth of the new
child has brought with it anxiety and a lack of
freedom in play and also nightmares. Neverthe-
less along with this there has come an acceptance of the mother as a separate person and
therefore establishment of herself with an identity and with a powerful bond with the father.
Presumably the "black mummy" is a relic of her

[3] For discussion of the term subjective object, see Winnicott (1971),
Playing and Reality, London: Tavistock Publications, p. 80. Also *The Matura-
tional Processes and the Facilitating Environment,* New York: International
Universities Press; London: Hogarth Press, 1965, pp. 180-181.

subjective preconceived notion about the mother.

When I go back over the details of the consultation I think the most important part happened early. It was when the Piggle responded to my interpretation about "another baby" by asserting her position as a baby in the cot, and then following this up with questions appropriate to the problem of the origin of babies. There is a maturity here which is not always so clearly demonstrable at the age of two years and five months.

The following are some of the important points to note of this consultation:

1. "I'm shy," is an evidence of ego strength and organization, and of the establishment of the analyst as a "daddy person."

2. Troubles started with the arrival of a new baby, which forced the Piggle into premature ego development.

She was not ready for simple ambivalence.

3. Indication of elements of madness: babacar, system *re* black, etc., nightmares.

4. Facility of communication.

5. Temporary resolution by regression to becoming the baby in the cot.

LETTER FROM THE PARENTS,
WRITTEN BY THE FATHER

"It was very good of you to see us; and it was a great help to be rung up just as we were wondering how best to communicate with you.

"As you know now, the day after the Piggle had been to you, she spent in the carrycot sucking a bottle. I did not feel that this satisfied her entirely at the time, and she soon gave up. She is now, alternately, the baby and the Big Mummy (a very indulgent one), but never herself; she will not allow us even to address her by her name. 'The Pigga' (she says) 'gone away. Is black. Both Piggas are black.'

"Bedtimes are still very difficult; she is usually awake at nine or ten, 'because of the babacar.' In the daytime, after having a good time, she has twice said: 'Cry Mummy' — 'Why?' — 'Because of the babacar.' The babacar seems usually linked with the black mummy; but the last few days, for the first time, a good mummy has come into the picture. The rather anxious and prim little voice, that does not seem her own, is not so much in evidence. She uses it mainly to talk about her baba — which is her doll, not her sister. With Susan, her sister ('the Sush Baba') she has a good relationship — she seems genuinely compassionate with her, in spite of the occasional ill-treatment, and they make rude noises together, to their great mutual pleasure. She mentioned several times, as if regretfully, that Dr. Winnicott does not know about the babacar, and said: 'Don't take me to London.' There was also something about having misinformed you that she came by car [she came by train; though I may have got the wrong end of the stick and I did not ask her.] Then for some days the subject was not men-

Negative transference — resistance

tioned, until she could not remember a song, and asked me to take her to Dr. W.: the next day, she asked me not to. Then she played taking trainloads of toys to London 'to play and to talk.' The last few days I had to be the Pigga, and she the Mummy: 'I'll take you to Dr. W. Say no.'—'Why?'—'Because I need you to say no.'

Ambivalence in transference

"The last two or three days she has asked me very intensely to take her to Dr. W.: the first time was when I said she seemed sad, she said she had been sad all the morning: 'Take me to Dr. W.' I said I would write and tell Dr. W. that she was sad. After a nightmare, last night (about the babacar, the black mummy who wanted her yams and made the Piggle black and made her neck hard) she said: 'The baba-car is'ite.' Asked what 'ite' meant, she said she would tell Dr. W. There is a new fantasy which she repeats with many elaborations, about everyone going splosh, splosh in the mud, or in 'moo's brrrrr.'

Reflection of the muddle of toys

"She is still often listless and sad, but has been playing more and has started to take more interest in things again, which we find encouraging.

"She is still very reserved with her father, compared with her behavior before Susan was born; she can only be tender, it seems, when she is being a baby. Whenever something exciting or new happens to her, or she meets someone new, she says that it has happened before, 'when I was a little baby in my carrycot.' We

overhear her at night, calling her baby and
speaking to her with great tenderness.

*Memory of
preambivalent
mother and
reproach to
present real
mother*

"I think that you were right that we had
been too 'clever' about understanding her
distress. We felt very involved and guilty about
not having arranged to not have a baby again so
soon and somehow, her nightly desperate pleading—'Tell me about the babacar'—made us
feel under pressure to say something meaningful.

"We never told you about her as a baby;
she seemed remarkably composed and sure of
touch, giving one the feeling that she had
authority within her world. We tried hard, and
I think successfully, to protect her from impingements which would make her world too
complicated. When Susan was born, Gabrielle
seemed somehow thrown out of her mold, and
cut off from her sources of nourishment. We
found it hurtful to see her so diminished and
reduced, and she may well have sensed this.
There was also a period of tension between us
two [the parents].

"Although, as you say, she is not managing
too badly, she does not quite seem to have
found her way back to herself. We thought you
might like to see some typical photos, which
may give a better idea to you than our description of what she seemed like to us."

LETTER FROM THE MOTHER

"I would like to send you a few more notes
before you see the Piggle.

"She seems to be managing very well now, and has come to realize things very reasonably and rather sadly. Overheard in bed: 'Don't cry little baby, the Sush Baba is here, the Sush Baba is *here.*' She says how nice it is to have a sister and so on; but I feel somehow she is managing at great cost to herself.

"She spends a lot of her time sorting and cleaning and washing—especially washing everything under the sun. Otherwise she does not play much, and is often at loose ends and a little sad. Quite a lot of time is spent making her baba [a doll, a highly idealized figure] comfortable.

"She is now much more often 'naughty,' e.g., kicks and screams at going to bed, etc. When she is angry, often gives up the ghost and says urgently: 'I am a baby, I am a baby'; has great difficulty in going to sleep at night, says, 'because of the babacar.'

Ego development in capacity to be naughty

"The babacar is 'taking blackness from me to you, and then I am frightened of you.' 'I am frightened of the black Pigga,' and 'I am bad' have come up quite often recently. (We are not in the habit of telling her that she is a bad girl and that sort of thing.) She is frightened of the black mummy and the black Pigga; she says: 'Because they make me black.'

"Yesterday she told me that the black mummy scratched my [the mother's] face, pulled off my yams, made me all dirty and killed me with 'brrrrr.' I said she must be longing to have a nice clean mummy again. She told me she had one when she was a little baby.

Reference to preambivalent subjective mother

"She seemed very pleased that you will see her. Sometimes when in difficulty talks about asking Dr. Winnicott. Still plays: 'You are the Piggle, I am the mummy, I'll take you to Dr. Winnicott, say no!'—'Why?'—'To tell him about the babacandle' (instead of babacar, with a little furtive smile, as if disguising babacar).

"(By the way, in case she is difficult to understand; she cannot pronounce R. Would say Yoman instead of Roman.)

Parents' lessened anxiety

"It is a great relief to us that you will see her. I think our knowing that you have matters in had, so to say, has made our behavior more natural, less unnaturally tolerant with her, which seems to be proving a good thing.

"She talks about going to see you, to tell you about the babacar. The babacar now seems to be carrying blackness from one person to the other."

EXTRACT FROM LETTER FROM FATHER

"A very paternal clergyman friend of mine came to tea some weeks ago and the Piggle was very shy. Yesterday, when talking of him, she said: 'I was very shy'—and I said he was 'a very daddy man' (the words she had used to describe him previously), and that this can make people feel shy. She was silent, and after a long time, said: 'Dr. Winnicott,' and then was silent again. That was that.[4]

---

[4] Further confirmation that the clue to Session 1 was: "I am shy."

SECOND CONSULTATION
(March 11, 1964)

The Piggle (two years, five months) arrived on the doorstep with her father (mother at home with Susan) and immediately took possession. She wanted to go into the consulting room, but this had to be postponed, so she went with her father to the waiting room. There the father and she were engaged in conversation. He was probably reading to her out of a book. When I was ready, she came along easily and went straight to the toys behind the door in the back half of the room. She took a little train and named it. Then she picked out the one new thing which was the blue eyebath of an Optrex bottle.

"What's this?" Then the train interested her: "I came in a train. What's this?" Again she said, "I came in a train." Her speaking was really clear to her parents who understood her language, but for me somewhat strange. She then took the little yellow electric light bulb we

played with last time and which has a face
drawn on it. She said: "Make it sick," and I had
to put a mouth on the top of it. Then she took a
bucket of toys and emptied them out. She
picked up a round toy with a perforated center
which came from goodness knows where.

"What's this? I haven't got one of these."
She then took a little truck and said: "What's
this? Do you know about the babacar?" Twice I
asked her to tell me what it was, but she was
unable to respond. "Was it the Piggle's car? Is it
the baby's car?" I then interpreted. I took a risk.
I said: "It's the mother's inside where the baby is
born from." She looked relieved and said: "Yes,
the black inside."

As if because of what she had said, she took
the bucket and deliberately overfilled it with
toys. I tried to find out what this was about by
interpreting in different ways. (She always
made a sign if she thought that I had said something good or bad.) The most popular interpretation seemed to be that this was a Winnicott
tummy, not a black inside. I said something
about being able to see what had got into there
and I remembered that last time I had talked in
terms of making a baby by filling up the bucket,
out of greedy eating. Because there was too
much in the bucket there was always something
falling down. This was a deliberately planned
effect. I interpreted that this was being sick, as
she had indicated by getting me to draw the big
mouth on the top of the electric light bulb. I
now began to see what was happening:

Me: Winnicott is the Piggle's baby; it's very greedy because it loves the Piggle, its mother, so much, and it's eaten so much that it's sick.

Piggle: The Piggle's baby has eaten too much. [She then said something about coming on the new train to London.]

Me: The new thing you want is about the Winnicott baby and the Piggle mother, about Winnicott loving the Piggle [mother], eating the Piggle, and being sick.

Piggle: Yes, you do.

It could be said that the work of the session was done.

There was now a lot of face play. She moved her tongue around; I imitated, and so we communicated about hunger and tasting and mouth noises, and about oral sensuality in general. This was satisfactory.

Nonverbal communication and interpretation

I said that it could be dark inside. Was it dark inside her tummy?

Me: Is the dark frightening?
Piggle: Yes.
Me: Do you dream about it being black inside?
Piggle: Piggle frightened.

Then there was a period in which the Piggle sat on the floor and was very serious. Eventually I said: "You like to see Winnicott." She answered: "Yes."

Consolidating the transference

We looked at each other a long time. She then went back to put more toys in the little bucket so that the sickness was played out again. She gave me the electric light bulb.

Piggle: Put in more eyes and more eyebrows.

These were already indicated very clearly and I made them even more clear. She then took another box and opened it. Inside she found animals. She immediately went over and took the two soft larger animals, a woolly lamb and a woolly faun. She placed the animals feeding from the box and she added some other toys to the little animals in the box: "They are eating their food." She half-covered the food box with the cover of the box. Here then was a kind of transitional phenomenon, in that in between her and me were the big woolly animals eating their food, the food being composed mostly of animals. I interpreted therefore as if she had told me this as a dream. I said: "Here is me the Winnicott baby come from the Piggle's inside born out of Piggle, very greedy, very hungry, very fond of Piggle, eating Piggle's feet and hands."

In the transference, Winnicott is the greedy, cannibalistic baby

I also tried the word "breast" among all the other part-objects. (I ought to have said "yams"). Piggle was standing seriously with one hand in her pocket. She then wandered right to the other end of the room which she associated with grownups. She took a long look at the window-box flowers, crocuses. Then she nearly went to the chair she associated with mother, but came over to the blue chair she associated with father. There she sat and said that she was being like daddy. I spoke again about Winnicott as the Piggle baby.

Me: Are you the mummy or the daddy?
Piggle: I am the daddy and the mummy too.

We watched the animals eating the food, and then she began to play with the door. She tried to shut it, but it did not shut easily (at the time the catch needed mending). Then she opened it and went to her father in the waiting room. I think I heard her say: "I am the mummy." There was now a lot of talk between her and her father, and I waited a long time without doing anything. At one point she came in with her father, carrying her hat which was a knitted affair, and did something that indicated she thought it might be time to go. It was clear that anxiety was operating. She then went back with her father to the waiting room. She then came in with her coat and said: "Going to go soon."

Needing father for communicating with me

She went back to the waiting room. I reread my notes. After five minutes, the Piggle ventured to come into the room and found me still sitting among the toys, near the bucket which was overfilled and "being sick over the floor all the time." She was very serious, and she said: "Can I have one toy?" I felt I knew where I was sufficiently clearly to take a line.

Doubt about her father's capacity to tolerate her ideas

Me: Winnicott very greedy baby; want all the toys.

Piggle not greedy— Winnicott infinitely greedy

She kept asking for just one toy, but I repeated what I was required to say in this game. Eventually she took one toy out to her father in the waiting room. I thought I heard her say: "Baby want all the toys." After a while she brought this toy back and she seemed very pleased that I was being greedy.

Piggle: Now the Winnicott baby has all the toys. I'll go to Daddy.
   Me: You are afraid of the greedy Winnicott baby, the baby that was born out of the Piggle and that loves the Piggle and that wants to eat her.

*Piggle
playing the
mother role*

She went to her father and tried to shut the door as she left. I heard the father working overtime in the waiting room trying to entertain her, because (of course) he did not know where he was in this game.

I told the father to come into the room now, and the Piggle came in with him. He sat in the blue chair. She knew what must be done. She got on his lap and said: "I am shy."

After a while she showed her father the Winnicott baby, this monster she had given birth to, and it was this that she was shy about: "And that's the food that the animals are eating." While performing acrobatics on her father's lap she told him all the details. Then she started a new and very deliberate chapter in the game. "I'm a baby too," she announced, as she came out head first onto the floor between her father's legs.

Me: I want to be the only baby. I want all the toys.

Piggle: You've got all the toys.

Me: Yes, but I want to be the only baby; I don't want there to be any more babies. [She got on her father's lap again and was born again.]

Piggle: I'm the baby too.

Me: I want to be the *only* baby [and, in a different voice], shall I be cross?

Piggle: Yes.

Born from daddy's body, as if it were mother's

I made a big noise, knocked over the toys, hit my knees and said: "I want to be the only baby." This pleased her very much, although she looked a little frightened, and she said to her father that it was the daddy and mummy lambs who were eating the food out of the trough. Then she went on with the game: "I want to be the baby too."

All this time she was thumb-sucking. Every time she was the baby she was born between her father's legs onto the floor. She called this "being born." Eventually she said: "Put the baby in the dustbin." I replied: "It's black in the dustbin." I tried to find out who was who. I found that it was I who was Gabrielle, and she was being the new babies, one after another, or the new baby reduplicated. At one point she said: "I've got a baby called Galli-galli-galli" (cf. Gabrielle). (Actually one of her dolls has this name.) She went on being born from father's lap onto the floor, and she was the new

Interchange of baby and Gabrielle roles

baby and I had to be cross, being the Winnicott
baby that came out of the inside and was born
out of the Piggle — and I had to be very cross
wanting to be the only baby.

"You're not to be the only baby," said the
Piggle. And then another baby was born, and
then another, and then she said: "I'm a lion,"
and made lion noises. I had to be scared because the lion would eat me. It seemed that the
lion was a return of my greediness as the Winnicott baby who wanted everything and wanted to
be the only baby.

Gabrielle answered positively or negatively
according to whether I was right or not, saying,
for instance: "Yes it is." Then there was a lion
baby.

Piggle: Yes it is [loud lion noises].

"I am just born. And it wasn't black inside." At this point I felt that I had been re-
warded for the interpretation I had made last
time when I said the black inside had to do with
hate of the new baby that was inside mother's
tummy. She had now developed a technique for
being the baby while allowing me to represent
herself.[1]

First relief from black phobia

There came a new development. She was
now having a different way of being born out of
the top of the father's head.[2] It was funny. I felt
sorry for father, and I asked him if he could

---

[1] The mother commented: "How strikingly the use of the transference emerges
in the knife edge between participation and interpretation."

[2] Being conceived of, i.e., born as an idea in the mind; wanted. D. W. W.

stand it. He replied: "O.K., but I would like to take my coat off." He was so hot. However, we were able to finish off at this point, because the Piggle had got what she came for.

"Where are the clothes?" and she put on her hat and coat and went home easily and in a very satisfied state.

COMMENTS

The following themes appeared in this session:

1. Having babies in terms of being sick.

2. Pregnancy as a result of oral greed, compulsive eating (split-off function).

3. Black inside, hate of the inside and contents.

4. Resolution in transference by Winnicott becoming the lost Gabrielle, so she could be the new baby, reduplicated.

Transitory identification with both parents.

5. Via Winnicott = Gabrielle = greedy = baby has its own rights.

6. Inside becomes *not black*.

7. Being conceived of, i.e., as in the mind. Mind being given localization in the head as if it were brain.

LETTER FROM THE MOTHER

Rediscovery of own identity, with return of playing

"When the Piggle came back from London she did not mention her visit, but played very

zestfully for the rest of the day. Altogether we
feel that she has been much freer since her last
visit to you; she sometimes plays on her own
again, and talks in what I take to be her own
voice.

"On going to bed, the day of her visit to
you, she said: 'Dr. baby was very cross, Dr. baby
kicked. I did not throw him in the Sinni ...
(corrected herself) in the duster (i.e., dustbin);
didn't put the lid on.'

"In the middle of the night she cried: her
'wee' was hurt, she said; she had to go to the
doctor. I said it was a bit red, either because of
her nappie, or because of being rubbed. She
said she had rubbed it, it goes d d d like a train,
it's what makes her frightened at night. It
makes her black. Then she talked of the black
mummy. I forget how it started, but it went on
with the black mummy saying: 'Where are my
yams?' — 'The yams are in the toilet, water rush-
ing down.' — 'The black mummy let me play
with her toys, made me baked custard with
raisins' (I had actually put raisins into baked
custard, which she greatly liked). She looked
very confused, and she said: 'I am angry with
mine daddy.' 'Why?' 'Because I love him too
much.'"

[I am puzzled about this recurring "goodness" of the "black mummy." It does not seem
linked with seeing a good and a bad mummy as
the same. Is it some sort of confusion between
the good and bad parts of herself? The theme of
placating the bad mummy recurs.]

*Erotic
excitement
and under-
lying oedipal
fantasies*

"The next evening she talked for a long time excitedly in bed, but I did not hear what she said.

"The morning after this she said to me: 'I went to London to see Dr. Winnicott. There was a great noise. Dr. W. very busy. He was a baby. I was a baby too. Didn't talk about the black mummy. He was a baby, very cross. The black mummy is very important for Dr. Winnicott.' Then she put a safety pin into the tap. 'I make it better with a pin.' Something about the water being able to come out again. To me: 'Did you come in and say it wasn't better?' I: 'That must have been in your dream.' 'Yes, you came and said it was not better; there was dirt in it.' Then something about the black mummy I did not quite hear.

Reference to clitoral masturbation

Perhaps reference to mental functioning

"I have been told frequently lately that the black mummy comes and makes me (mother) black. At bedtime I have to 'ring up' the black mummy and the black Sush Baby. The conversation is confined to 'Hullo.'

This reminds me: a day or two before she went to see you (she having complained of nightmares about the black mummy) I asked her: 'Did you sleep well? Did the black mummy come?' — 'The black mummy doesn't come, the black mummy is inside me.'"

ANOTHER LETTER FROM THE MOTHER

"We are going away in the middle of April for about three weeks.

"The Piggle has been very persecuted by the 'black mummy.' She has been having nightmares, and does not go to sleep till all hours.

" 'I didn't tell Dr. Winnicott about the black mummy because he is very busy. Dr. Winnicott very busy, he was a baby. I would be frightened to tell Dr. W. about the black mummy. He was very cross, he was a baby. I was a baby too. I would be shy to tell Dr. W. about the black mummy.'

"Her chief complaint about the black mummy is that she makes the Piggle black, and then the Piggle makes everyone, even the daddy, black.

"Last night she woke up 'frightened of the black mummy' and asked her father to 'give the black mummy raisins' (the Piggle particularly likes raisins).

"She also woke up frightened of the black Sush Baby, who makes her black. (The day before she had pushed Susan over, which somewhat alienated public opinion.) The black Sush Baba comes fairly frequently and has to be rung up before she goes to sleep. (The Sush Baba is a reference to Susan.)

"The Piggle is rather less often the mummy or the baby now. She is much naughtier in the sense of refusing to go to bed, etc., but usually rather miserably so. There is one more thing: 'Baby bablan'—this is signed on all the letters she writes and drawings she makes; it has to be put on envelopes. I have no idea what it means.

Greater tendency to be herself

I think I told you that the Piggle's baby is called
"Gaby-Gaby" which I think is "Gabrielle,"
which she cannot pronounce. [Baby Gobla
(not bablan). I would think this is another version of Gabrielle, like Galy-Galy or Galli-Galli
—I don't know in what way the two versions
differ.]"

FURTHER LETTER FROM THE MOTHER

"The Piggle asked to see you, it seemed
rather urgently. When I said there may not be
enough time before going away to France, she
said very fiercely that there was.
"She woke this morning in a real destructive fury, tearing up anything in sight, and then
retired to her carrycot saying she wanted to see
Dr. Winnicott. Then she got inside my dressing
gown (which I was wearing) and told me something about dreaming that the black mummy
had eaten her. Then she emerged and asked me
about being born. I told her, as often before,
how she came out, was wrapped in a towel and
was handed to me. 'And you dropped me.'—
'I didn't.'—'Yes you did. The towel was made
dirty.'
"She has been a bit miserable lately. I
think it may be a great strain for her to be with
us quite so much; there are few children
around. I am looking for a nursery school that
will have her one or two mornings a week. Most
of them will only take her every day, and that
would be too much I think.

LETTER FROM THE FATHER

"We would like to let you have some notes on the Piggle. She has been in a state of great agitation and anxiety for the last few days and has been saying things such as: 'I'm very worried. I want to see Dr. Winnicott.' When asked why, she always says it is because of the 'baba-car,' the 'black mummy,' or the 'black mummy's yams.' She is also frightened of the black Sush Baba (= Susan): 'I made her black.' This also said about the black mummy. She still repeats frequently, before going to bed: 'The Black Mummy says: "Where are my yams?" '; and one morning after this, she asked to drink out of her mother's breasts.

"Almost every morning, she wants to go inside her mother's dressing gown, or be rolled up 'roly-poly' in a rug. She seems to be suffering greatly from what was once called a 'sense of sin.' She is greatly worried when she breaks or soils anything; sometimes she will go round murmuring to herself: 'Never mind, never mind,' in a little, artificial voice — also, when she kicks Susan, to whom she is remarkably responsive, despite occasional lapses. She objected to clothes we bought her because 'there is too much white: I want a black jersey.' She said she could wear black clothes, as she was black and bad.

Depressive anxiety

Black linked with sense of guilt

"We took notes on her yesterday, though it was not a typical day. She was worse than usual, and she was with us all day. On most days, our help, called by her 'the Wattie,' an elderly

woman, spends the morning with us. She is very
attached to 'the Wattie.'

"In the morning, she handed us her beloved Teddy, having made a hole in his leg, and
taken all the stuffing out; and she was very
distressed by this. All day long, she kept asking
desperately for things that we do not usually
deny her, as if she had to fight a great battle to
obtain them from us. She told her mother that
she wanted to get married. When told that it
might be a good idea to wait, she said most
intensely, 'No, no, I'm a big girl *now*,' and
implied that she was too old for toys.

"Going to bed created a major scene — as
happens quite often now. She says she is frightened of the black mummy coming after her. At
10 P.M. she had all the bedclothes on the floor.
She got out of bed and insisted on taking her
chair next door. I said that it was hers, and that
it only needed a cushion: 'A black cushion: then
I can sit on it.' — 'Because you are black?' — 'Yes.
Because I broke the black mummy into pieces.
I am worried.' — 'Don't.' 'I want to worry. My
bottom is sore: can I have some white cream?' A
prayer, a recent introduction, and asking mainly for protection, has to be repeated again and
again.

Added note: " 'I clear Dr. Winnicott's toys
away, in case I break them.' The Piggle said this
when she came to see you last time, in the taxi. I
forgot to tell you at the time."

*This play
appears in
a later
session*

*Flight from
immaturity
to the idea
of adulthood*

*Guilt
relative to
compulsive
destruction*

*Magic
employed
to ward off
frightening
ideas*

THIRD CONSULTATION
(April 10, 1964)

The Piggle (two years, six months) looked less tense than before, and this state remained constant. She seemed one stage further removed from the actual anxieties that she talked about. In fact, I realized now how much she had been *in* them before, like a psychotic child. I went to the waiting room and found her with her "baby" which is a little doll with diaper and safety pin. She was shy to follow me into the consulting room, so I went in alone. Then I went to fetch her and she showed me a bag in which she had put sand and a stone. This was taken from the street. She would not come in so I said: "Daddy come too" (which was what she wanted). She brought in the bag with the sand and the stone, leaving the baby. The father sat in his seat in the grown-up half of the room, and for half the time he and we two were separated by the curtain. She went straight for the toys and did exactly the same as last time.

Symbol of despair about becoming pregnant like an adult

Piggle: What's this for?

    Me: That's the one you asked about last time and I said about it: "Where did the baby come from?"

I asked about the stone and the sand: "Where did it come from?"

Piggle: From the sea.

    She took other objects and the bucket and obviously remembered everything. She went over all the details:

Piggle: What's this? A train. An engine. Rail carriages. Trucks.

    She called one a "little lion." Then she took the little boy.

Piggle: Have you another little boy?

    She found a little man and his wife.

Piggle: I like this [the boy].

    I had to help make him sit up. Then another engine.

Piggle: I came on a train to London to see Winnicott. I want to know why the black mummy and the babacar.

    Me: We will try to find out about it.

    I left it at that. She went on choosing toys, the Red Indian (which is blue plastic).

Piggle: I haven't got one of these cars.

She was putting all the toys out, arranging them side by side:

Piggle: I wonder what this is. Have you got any
boats? I can't find anywhere for this one
to sit on [a plastic sitting figure].
Winnicott not to be a baby; be a Winnicott. Yes it did frighten me. Not be a
baby again.

She was obviously toying with the idea of repeating the game of last time.

Piggle: Can I empty everything out of the
bucket?
Me: Yes. That was the baby being sick when
Winnicott was a baby.

She then talked about the truck for holding things. Then another train. She took two cars the same as each other and compared them and put them together.

Me: Not like the Piggle and the baby because Piggle is bigger than the baby.

She put many of the toys side by side, continuing:

Piggle: What's this? An engine. I came in a
taxi. Did you go in a taxi? Two taxis.
To see Winnicott. To work with Winnicott.

*Assertion that
we work. Play
at this stage is
communica-
tion, not for
pleasure*

She then tried to get me to try to blow up the balloon which I think she left with me the first time she came. I did not have much success. She rubbed the balloon in her hands, showed me her zipper, and said: "Up and down again." She again urged me to blow up the balloon. She said she had a pen, possibly a reference (the only one) to my writing with a pencil, taking notes. Here she found the little animals in one box, which made her want the dog, and she reached for it. It was not within sight, but she remembered the two big soft animals from the last time. She put them together, side by side, and pushed them down on to the floor (she called them both dogs, although one was a fawn).

Piggle: One dog was cross.

Both the dogs were going to meet the train, and she squashed them down into the floor ruthlessly.

Anxiety about ruthlessness, or compulsive behavior

Piggle: Have you another dog?
  Me: No.

She went to show daddy three train cars. She had a conversation with him in which she said something about all kinds of colors, and then she dropped the toys and said: "Dropping train." She was showing that it was deliberate and indicating defecation. She then came over to me and tried to put the little man and woman into the car.

Piggle: Too big to go in. One day must find a little man.
  Me: A boy baby instead of a daddy?

She went over to daddy and started to use him, and I pulled back the curtain that hid him so that he was more part of the toy situation. She walked up her father, and he (knowing that he was in for a strenuous time) took his coat off. She got right above his head with him holding her (last time's game had now come back).

Piggle: I be a baby. I want to be bryyyyyh.

This, I learned, meant feces. (The father said Susan played this game of being held up above his head and Piggle was very intrigued and has often enjoyed copying the baby. It was as if she denied the fact that she was really too heavy for this game.)

Piggle: I am the Piggle.

Gradually she began to get born down onto the ground, between daddy's legs.

Piggle [to me]: You can't be a baby because it makes me very frightened.

From primary to secondary process

Somehow she managed to keep control of the situation so that she was *playing at it rather than being in it*. Last time she was in it. Eventually, I said: "Shall I be a cross Piggle?" She replied: "Be cross now." So I was, and I upset the toys. She came along and picked them all up.

Piggle: What are you angry about?
   Me: I wanted to be the only baby so I was sick. Mummy got a bryyyyyh baby.

Piggle: Mummy hasn't got bryyyyyh, only wee-
        wee.

She then talked about the Piggle's baby: "I
call my baby Gaddy-gaddy-gaddy" (cf. Gabrielle, Baby-baby, Galli-galli-galli).

The father said this probably has to do
with Gabrielle. She was referring to the baby
doll in the waiting room. She helped us out by
saying: "Girlie-girlie-girlie," giving an addition-
al meaning to the word, and she started to have
the idea of going home (anxiety).

*Preference for
genital over
pregenital
pregnancy
ideas*

Me: These things make you feel frightened
        because I was a cross baby.
Piggle: Be very cross! [And I was. I talked about
        a bryyyyyh baby.]
Piggle: No, a Sush Baby.
Me: I [I = Piggle = baby] wanted daddy to
        give me a baby.
Piggle [to her father]: Will you give Winnicott a
        baby?

I talked about Piggle being angry, shutting
her eyes, not seeing the mummy who had become black because she was angry with her because daddy gave mummy a baby.

Piggle: In bed in the night I get very fright-
        ened.
Me: A dream?
Piggle: Yes, a dream; a black mummy and a
        babacar coming after me.

At this point she picked up a wheel with a

pointed axle — it came off one of the trains —
and she put the pointed axle in her mouth.

Piggle: What's this? [It could be said that she
was taking the only dangerous thing
among the toys and relating it to her
mouth.]

Me: If the black mummy and the babacar
caught you would they eat you?

All the time she was tidying up, and was
distressed because she could not put the top on
one of the boxes. There was too much in the
box.

Me: When you had the dream, what were
daddy and mummy doing?

Piggle: They were downstairs with Renata eating broccoli [Renata was the new *au
pair* girl.] Renata likes broccoli and
supper.

All the time the Piggle continued putting
everything away tidily.

Me: Have we found out about the black
mummy and the babacar?

Piggle: No. I want to come to my baby [doll];
will you wait a minute?

She was playing with the door.

Piggle: Be a Winnicott. Daddy will look after
you. Will you Daddy? If I close the
door, Winnicott will be frightened.

Me: I would be frightened of the black
    mummy and the babacar.

She then shut the door as near as she could
and went to get the baby. When she came back,
I said I was frightened of the black mummy and
the babacar, but daddy had looked after me.
After coming back there was a lot of play with
this (doll) baby, and the words "open" and
"shut" now referred to the doll's diaper and its
huge safety pin. Father helped here. She took a
long time putting on the diaper.

Piggle: Do you want a baby Winnicott? You
    can have mine later.

Daddy went on supervising the diapering
technique and helping.

Piggle: Don't shut it [the pin].

She then had a secret conversation with
father about giving cake and pie to the baby.
She said: "She's a very bryyyyyh baby" (which
meant that she had made a mess and was being
changed). She then came over and showed me
her black thumb which she had evidently
caught in something. Then she took two toy
umbrellas out of her pocket and put one in my
hair. She picked up her baby and put the two
umbrellas in the baby's hair. She tried to sit the
baby in the little chair, but got jealous of it and
sat there herself. She then wanted to show the
baby how funny she looked in the mirror.

Me: The baby is Winnicott.

Piggle: No, Gaddy-gaddy-gaddy.

She was now ready to go, with everything tidied up. She fetched her father's coat for him to put on, and collected the sand, and the stone which was in the bag.

> *Me:* All right, but have we understood about the black mummy and the babacar?

She looked at all the toys which were carefully put away and said: "The babacar is all tidied up." And it seemed to me as if she were saying the babacar has to do with bryyyyyh and wee-wee belonging to the black mummy who is black because she has been hated since daddy gave her a baby.

Forgetting in defense against muddle and anxiety

I remained sitting on the floor, and she went quite happily out the front door with her father.

COMMENTS

The following themes were the highlights of this session:

1. Pick up on the last time's game, but *delay* associated with anxiety.

2. New ability to *play at* (thus coping with) rather than *to be in* the frightening fantasy—(a) relief and increased range, (b) loss of direct experience.

3. Going to meet anxiety through the dangerous pointed axle, in her mouth, suggested a fantasy of the mother's oral greedy experience of the father's penis.

4. Now her baby (the doll) gave her some place as a girl with mother identification = self.

5. Partial resolution on basis of black having to do with hate around the subject of daddy giving mummy a baby, but somewhat intellectualized.

6. The dark was packed away, i.e., forgotten.

7. Importance of my not *understanding* what she had not yet been able to give me clues for. Only she knew the answers, and when she could encompass the meaning of the fears she would make it possible for me to understand too.

LETTER FROM THE MOTHER

"I would like to send you a few notes about the Piggle, though I think my husband told you some of them on the 'phone.

"She came home from her session in a foul mood; and the next few days were full of scenes, especially about going to bed. Now she seems to have settled down again.

"For several days she wanted to be Susan's baby—a most frustrating situation, as Susan does not respond; when asked why: 'I'm trying to *like* the Sushbaba.'

"For a day or two after her session she was very aggressive to other children. She has a glove puppet, and said to me about it: 'Make him shy, then I can hit him.'

"The evening after her session, she told

me: 'I am frightened of the black mummy. I have to go to Dr. Winnicott again, the new Dr. Winnicott.' She always refers to her sessions in this formal way, except that just before she came to see you last she chanted: 'Winnicott, Winnicott' in a rather affectionate way.

"She said several times now that she must go to Dr. W. because of the black mummy. 'Why, did you not tell Dr. W.?' 'No, I told him about the babacar.' 'Is that where babies come from? The babacandle, by candlelight.'

"She complained about her wee being sore. 'Did you rub it or was it the nappie?' — 'Rub it. It's black. Give me some *white* cream to make it better. Then I can rub it again.'

"We watched the darkness come down over the mountains. 'When it's dark, I shall be frightened. Dr. W. does not know that I am frightened of the dark.' — 'Why, did you not tell him?' — 'I packed all the dark away.'

"For a few days after the session I was a very black mummy indeed. She did not believe anything I said. She broke several things, especially the sugar bowl from which she constantly helped herself to 'big sugars,' although this is forbidden. She seems to feel terrible about any kind of destruction she brings about if it cannot be immediately repaired, even if it is insignificant. Since my mother is staying with us it is she who tends to be the black mummy, so the Piggle and I get on well. Then I am the Piggle and she is the mummy. She is not quite so solicitous and careful now. Two conversations yesterday: 'Pigga, do you like me?' — Me: 'Yes.' She: 'Do you remember when I broke the dish?' — She: 'Do you like me?' — Me: 'Yes. And you?' — 'No, I don't like you. You are black, and then you will make me black.' "

LETTER FROM THE MOTHER,
WRITTEN FROM HOLIDAY ABROAD

"We want to write to you again because we are very worried about the Piggle, and we would like you to think about whether she may not need a full analysis — though we don't quite know how we could arrange it if she does.

"What most worries us is the narrowing of her experience; she seems quite imprisoned in her own world, as if inaccessible to outside experience. The only thoughts that preoccupy her other than continuously wanting things, and the appearance of her person, are her memories (usually hearsay ones, family saga) of when she was a baby and could not speak.

Deterioration. Rigidity of organized defenses

"Her speech is increasingly conducted in an artificial little voice, and she is becoming increasingly affected and ungenuine. She now goes to great lengths to draw attention to herself, often creating dramatic scenes.

Illness now organized. True self hidden

"She is still very frightened at night — talks less about it now before going to bed — however wakes several times at night, sometimes crying.

Expulsion of own evil

"She is crying, she says, because the dark will make her black. (Once she walked into my room to see whether I was black.) In the night she seems to remember all the injuries she wrought during the day. (She has a tendency now to lightning acts of aggression, such as throwing a stone at my head, or hitting Susan's hand with a tray.) 'Does Susan's hand hurt?' 'Is your head broken?' 'Give me a needle to mend my blanket.' 'Do you want to mend my head?' 'I can't mend you, you are too hard.'

Depressive anxiety

"Another time in the night she said: 'Do you remember when the doctor pricked me?' (injection). 'I must go to the doctor, I am ill. It's here' — pointing to her wee."

Masturbation fantasies

LETTER FROM THE MOTHER,
AFTER RETURNING HOME

"I should like to tell you more about the Piggle.

"In some way that I cannot define, I feel that she is better; she has gone through a period when she was bored, listless and discontented, and at times wantonly destructive — tearing things up or breaking or soiling them. Now she gives one more the feeling of living her life, and she is less mannered and unnatural.

Family setting had provided the mental hospital in which she could reach to her illness

"I had not realized previously how much she is haunted by guilt and the responsibility for her destructiveness. She mentions in a most agonized manner breakages of weeks ago that I hardly took any notice of at the time. I smacked her when she persistently tried to lift my skirts in a shop, and then forgot about it. Two weeks later she said: 'Mummy, I won't lift your skirt again.' Or: When I carried Susan, her baby sister, I knocked her against the door and she cried. The Piggle: 'That was your fault.' I: 'Yes, that was my fault.' Piggle, very concerned: 'Will you dream about it now?' She is as worried as ever at night, about being made black by the black mummy and the babacar.

"Talk about dead things has lately become prominent. Last night she very urgently wanted to tell me about the black mummy. It started in the usual sing-song voice: 'The black mummy says: where are my yams, where are my yams?' Then: 'The black mummy has got a seaside and a swing.' (I had taken her to the seaside for the first time, and she loves swings.) I said she did not seem to want the black mummy to have such good things? She: 'No, I want to spoil them. I want to spoil your things.' Then she said I had big yams and she wanted them. Then she seemed to get mixed up and said I wanted her yams, and looked very confused. I said she had small yams, and when she was bigger she would have big ones. 'Yes, when I can cook.' (I had told her when I came in that I must hurry, as I was cooking supper for daddy and myself.) I: 'You have already started to be able to cook; you did make a baked custard.' She: 'Yes I can only cook dead things.' Then she said: 'Life is difficult' (copying my phrase); 'It hurts me' (her own addition).

Melancholic depression

"She mentions you occasionally rather casually, e.g., suddenly says she wants to go and play with Dr. W.'s toys and tell him about the

black mummy; or making a village, one house is
Dr. W.'s home."

LETTER FROM THE MOTHER

"This is to confirm that the Piggle will
come with her father to see you.

"For two days running now she has asked to
suck my 'yams' (breasts) after she had gone to
bed at night. She asked with such intensity that
I let her. I: 'Why?' 'I want to suck them like a
lollipop.' Afterward she asked me for something
she could suck and chew and that then would go
down into her tummy. Then she was frightened
of the black mummy again and wanted to go to
Dr. Winnicott. When I told her the day she was
going, she said: 'And the day after and the day
after that.' When I had gone out I heard heart-
broken crying: 'I want my baby, my baby, my
Galli-galli-baby" (Galli-galli baby is the name
of her baby doll, around which much of her
activities used to pivot, though no longer as
much now, and it is also her way of pro-
nouncing her own name, Gabrielle, which she
has not yet been able to pronounce properly.)"

FOURTH CONSULTATION
(May 26, 1964)

As I learned later by phone Gabrielle (now two years, eight months) spent the journey in the train curled up on her father's lap sucking his thumb.

She went straight to the muddle of toys, talking: "It's warm in here. We came by train. Have you seen...."

She took the little boats and put them on the carpet. She reached for one of the big soft dogs. She was joining up engines with carriages. Then, spontaneously, she said: "I came about the babacar."

Conscious need for help— specific problem

I helped her here with her attempts to link the parts of some trains. She arranged the toys in some way which was not specific enough for me to understand. She said: "The window (of the room) isn't open." When I opened it she said: "We opened the window here."

We resumed the work we had started.

Piggle: Isn't this a nice car! I like coming here very much. I came by train. Is daddy waiting for me? Two rooms, one for daddy and one for me. The train did shake and shake and shake.

She took a little wooden fence and broke it and shoved the stick into the saloon car through its window. This was a very deliberate operation. I said something about a daddy trying to make babies (using the car as a mummy). She broke off two bits of wood.

Piggle: Isn't the room warm! On holiday it was warm. We got brown. The baby was brown, Susan baby brown, my sister. She does crawl upstairs. She wets on the potty now.

Me: She is growing up isn't she!

Resort to objectivity

She said something about "growing up," and she was handling the car. She said: "Be a baby. Take all the cars away." She was having some game here with the cars, naming their colors.

Piggle: Two cars Mr. Winnicott. You are Mr. Winnicott!!

There was something here she wanted to throw away.

Piggle: Did you hear the nightingale? It's a pity that you moved so far away. [This had to do with the fact that she was only just beginning to understand that I was not a near neighbor.] Do you remember. . . .

Flirtatious romance: father transference

Me: It's a long time since you wanted me.

Piggle: Cos I like you to blow up the balloon. [There was the old degenerated balloon which she spent a long time playing with in a desultory sort of way, and sometimes I helped her.] Here's a church with a top [spire] on it.

She arranged the church with a car at each end. Then she became interested in an object which in fact she could not know about. It was a broken-off, flat, circular object that was originally a humming top.

Piggle: Where does this come from? [This had come into the first session.]

Me: I don't know.

She was smiling and there was something to do with a rocking cradle with toys arranged to illustrate.

Piggle: Isn't the room warm! Piggle's got a cotton jersey with a zip. [To illustrate this she pulled the zip and banged her elbow on the door. It was a little bang. She thought the hurt was rather fun.]

Piggle took boats of various colors, and she said the white one was pink. She tried to make the boats stand up upside down, which was impossible (indeterminate play). I said somewhere here: "Why do you like me?" And she said: "Because you tell me about the babacar." I had a conversation with her about this because I had said the word wrong, and it was clear that I had not understood properly. I wanted her to help to sort things out in my own mind.

Piggle: There is the black mummy.

We tried to work out something about whether the black mummy was cross or not. She was making a car go to-and-fro. There was something here that I reintroduced, something to do with mummy being angry with Gabrielle because Gabrielle was angry with mummy for having a new baby. And then mummy seemed to be black. All this was rather vague. She was playing on her own with the toys, *allotting various cars to me or to herself.*

First sign of the me-not-me theme

Piggle: My shoes are too small; I'll take them off.

I helped a little. There was something about feet growing.

Piggle: I am growing into a big big girl [and she went on:] pi pi pi [etc., talking to herself]. There's a pretty lady waiting for the car, a nice lady to come for the children. The black mummy is naughty.

Manifestation of anxiety probably due to oedipal fears

She looked for an engine and put it into something, and there was the idea of a big one and a baba one.

Piggle: Shall we pack up and put everything away [anxiety]? That goes down there.

She threw away a water lily into the waste-

paper basket. (This water lily, made by someone else from paper, was a carry-over from last
session.) She tidied up all the toys. There was
no manifest anxiety; she took her shoes and
walked down the passage to daddy in the waiting room. For some minutes I could hear them
talking in the waiting room.

*Delayed
rejection of
this evidence
of my seeing
other children*

Piggle: I want to go, please let me go.

And so on. I was making note of the considerable personality growth with coherence appearing and, for the first time, something that could
be called poise. I would say that she was happy.
She came in to say goodbye. Daddy was trying
to persuade her to stay, saying: "No, you can't
go yet."

*Note poise as
an infant
(Parent's let-
ter, January 4,
1964)*

Piggle: I want to go.

I got daddy to sit down on the chair in the
other half of the room, and she got onto daddy's
lap. Now the game developed again in which
she was a baby being born out of daddy, between his legs. This was done over and over
again. It was a big physical strain on her father,
but he carried on unself-consciously doing exactly what he was told to do. I said to her that it
was important that she had father when she was
frightened of being alone with Winnicott and
wanting to play something like this with Winnicott, using a man as a mother to be born out of.
Father's shoes came into all this a great deal,
with a conflict about his having them on or off;
soon they were on the floor, and she was cling-

*Recovery from
reaction to
impingement
(failure of
ego courage)*

*Shoes as
breast symbols*

ing to father: I was saying: "I don't know about babacars."

Piggle was being very positive toward her father, kneeling up and sucking his thumb (I didn't know at this stage that she had been sucking his thumb on the way up, curled up in his lap in the train). I said that she was scared because of the game in which I had become the angry Piggle. By this time father had got his coat off and was trying to cope in shirtsleeves.

Me: Winnicott is the angry Piggle and the Piggle was being the baby born using daddy instead of mummy. She was frightened of me because she knew how angry I must be, and the new baby was sucking daddy's thumb [i.e., mummy's breast].

She looked at me in a particular way and I said: "Have I become black?" She thought a lot and said: "No," and she shook her head.

Me: I am the black mummy.
Piggle: No [playing with daddy's tie].

There was a lot of jerking and sucking of father's thumb, and I made a rather definite interpretation to do with her wanting daddy all to herself so that mummy turns black, which means angry. I seem to have said: "She wants to put Gabrielle in the dustbin" (risky remark). She appeared pleased about this, and went on playing with daddy's tie, trying to do it up. She said something about pretending that the black

Father used as mother in the transference, releasing me for other functions

Reassurance by reminding herself that this mother was actually a man

Now father is being the real father

mummy wasn't there, and this had something
to do with the dark night. She had undone
father's other shoe and, if allowed, would have
undressed him altogether. Along with this, was
the idea of making mummy go black. I said
something about being born again, this time
from daddy. About now daddy was doing up his
shoes and Gabrielle was getting up on to his
back.

Alternative theme develops, with father as father and analyst as jealous mother

Piggle: Can I climb up you again?

I kept on saying: "Making mummy go black."
Gabrielle then said quite definitely: "Mummy
wants to be daddy's little girl."

Second theme established. Clue to session

She had plenty of energy and would have
gone on with this kind of game, but daddy had
had enough, and began to say no. It was very
hot weather. It was also near the end of the time
I had allotted her.

Me: The black mummy is now Winnicott,
and he is going to send the Piggle away.
He is going to put the Piggle in the
wastepaper basket, like the water lily.

I began to be undecided about calling her the Piggle or Gabrielle at this stage, because of the me-not-me theme that had been introduced

The session ended, and she was very friendly. I stayed where I was, being the black angry
mummy *who wanted to be daddy's little girl
and was jealous of Gabrielle.* At the same time I
was Gabrielle being jealous of the new baby
with mother. She ran to the door, they went off
and she waved. Her last words were: "Mother
wants to be daddy's little girl." And this became
the main interpretation of the session.

By phone that evening, I learned about her having come curled up and sucking daddy's thumb. After the session, she changed into a more grown-up girl. She was at ease and very happy. Moreover she was observing everything on the way home, seeing cats and other animals, eating food and giving no trouble. She had become openly positive in her relation to her father and had lost the regressive behavior. In the evening she played constructively in a way that she had not been doing recently. Her uncle came, and at first she was shy, but then she was very nice and friendly. Eventually, going to bed, she said out of the blue: "I don't know who is uncle Tom and who is daddy."

Relief resulting from work done in the session

I thought that it was possible to see in this her growing ability to let people stand for basic father-mother figures, and that the remark had reference to the way she used me and her father according to how she wanted to use us so that we changed roles as the game altered. In other words, what mattered was communication — the experience of being understood. At the back of all this is a sense of security with regard to the fact of her real father and mother.

It could be said that there had now developed a wider area for play experience, involving cross-identification, etc. In the compulsive acting, there had been a series of acts of *becoming* mother, father, baby, etc., so that enjoyable playing was out of the question. Now pleasure in playing had arrived. This release of fantasy made for greater freedom in communication and in the exploration of bad, black, destructive, and other ideas.

COMMENTS

The following are the main themes brought up in this session:

1. In train coming, curled up on father's lap sucking his thumb (I did not know this).

2. Dramatization of male sexual sadistic act.

3. Idea of natural growth, maturation.

4. Sense of distance between us in intervals between sessions (end of denial).

5. Idea evolving of mummy being angry with Gabrielle for being daddy's little girl — superimposes on idea of Gabrielle's anger with the new babies born out of daddy.

6. Urethral erotism, clitoral excitement and masturbation evident as functional basis for some of the fantasy formation, and as part of the search for information.

LETTER FROM THE MOTHER

"The Piggle has asked several times to see you, and yesterday in her play she took train-loads of toys to London. She suggested staying with her grandmother (called La-la-la) who lives near London. She took about three hours to go to sleep. For a few days now she would not let me kiss her, in case I make her black; but she has been much more affectionate toward me,

and has kissed me spontaneously, which she has
never done before. The other night, she told me
that I was a nice mummy, and then proceeded
to scrape me. She said she was scraping the
black off, and then she tried to blow it off the
pillow.

"Every evening there is the same ceremony:
'Shall I tell you about the babacar.... The
black mummy says, "Where are my yams?" '
(breasts). Once I asked impatiently: 'Well,
where are they?'—'In the toilet, with holes.' She
is very preoccupied with yams. Yesterday she
said out of the blue: 'Pity my yams have no milk
in them.' When I say good night to her she often
buttons up my cardigan so that my yams don't
get 'dirty and dead.' She has been very preoccupied with 'dead' lately. I said once: 'Soon your
yams will grow.'—She: 'And yours will die.'

"After being to you, she said, very resolved,
that she would not go to London any more.
When asked why, she said that Dr. Winnicott
does not want me to climb up the daddy. By the
way, this climbing up the daddy is something
she never did at home when she was a baby; it
was what her sister, the Sush Baba did, and it
seemed to amuse the Piggle greatly.

"She said to me on another occasion: 'I
tried several times to climb up the daddy. Dr.
Winnicott said "No." ' She said that Dr. W.
knew about the babacar.

"The evening of her visit to you she said
that she could not tell the difference between
Tom—her much-loved uncle, whom she has

only seen about three times—and the daddy. Later, she said: 'Daddy, Tom, and Dr. Winnicott are all daddy-men; isn't it funny!' Out of the blue, she said to her daddy: 'Dr. W. has funny toys.' Then again: 'I can't tell the difference between my toys and the Sush Baba's toys. Very funny toys.'

"She has had a fantasy lately, repeated for two evenings, that if the daddy is in the kitchen, the bottles are broken—the bottle of Rose Hip Syrup (immensely popular) and the Sush Baba's bottle—there would be glass everywhere, and the Piggle would tread on it.

Male function equated with aggression, fear of female identification, which means being broken

"Generally, in herself, she has been very depressed occasionally, and also wantonly destructive and messy. This alternates with periods of reasonableness well above her age and station, and a great deal of washing and ordering—which stands out in our very casual family.

Depression as evidence of unit-self, toward acknowledging own aggressive impulse. Within the depression fantasy is hidden chaos, which turns into tidiness in phases of behavior

FIFTH CONSULTATION
(June 9, 1964)

Gabrielle was now two years, nine months old, and Susan was one year old.

It was a hot day, and we had the window open. This brought the external world in at various moments. My notes are relatively obscure because of the heat and my sleepiness.

She was busy with the toys, the father was in the waiting room. She took the toys out.

Piggle: Everything is falling out. I got one of these. I got a lot of nice toys [handling a fence]. You didn't have a holiday.

Me: I did.

Piggle: I've got a nice sister. Goes away in her bag for sleeping in. So many trains. Why? [She was fixing a train and needed help; it really was difficult.] I'm getting bigger and bigger. I'm going to be three. How old are you?

Me: I'm sixty-eight.

She repeated "sixty-eight" five times.

67

Piggle: I like you to be near us [implying the distance between my house and hers was too great]. Shall I be three and a baby who likes playing—a good baby who doesn't be sick? [Here was a reminder of the sickness represented by the bucket, spilling over with toys. She was examining a figure.] Yes I like playing with the toys. Baby throws my toys away.

Probably also a reference to the great difference in age

She was making various tentative arrangements of the toys (interrupted to listen to a horse and cart on the road). She put the churches in a row (interrupted by "oo, oo" sounds of pigeons).

Impingements because of open window (failure of ego support)

Piggle: Horrid noises.

She was contemplating here.

Me: These things disturb you while you work.

Piggle: My shoes are too hot.

Here she undid the double straps. She did this on her own, which was quite a feat.

Piggle: My toes—ten toes. It is sandy.

Me: In France?

Piggle: No.

A plane passed over, and this interrupted her playing again. She said: "I've been in a plane."

She had arranged four houses and two houses and had put the two churches away, and so on. Anxiety began to show in the form of: "Is daddy ready to go? Daddy's tired." (This was a reference to last time.) I answered: "He's resting in the waiting room."

There were now teeth noises and I asked what she was biting.

Piggle: Do you like bread and butter?
  Me: Here it's like eating a meal.
Piggle: Goosey goosey gander [reciting this through]. Here's a funny toy [again the remains of an old humming top]. Shall I bang it on the floor or not?

She banged it on her button: "I can hear some water tipping, tipping, tipping" (meaning dropping, a noise of dropping water from up-stairs, coming down the pipe). She took the bucket: "There are not many toys in here. Shall I fill it up till it's full up?"

The sickness— result of compulsive greediness

I made a remark here about feeling hungry and feeling less hungry if full up, and not enjoying eating, but stuffing in order to keep hunger away. She placed the houses in a row and said: "Who lives here? A little man, a lady too—Mrs. Winnicott."

Compulsive behavior, control of split-off function

Here she put a shoe on and did it up: "I'm going back to my mummy"—and she gave the address. I replied: "So you will be with mummy and daddy." She resumed play as if anxiety had gone, this having to do with the idea of Mrs. Winnicott (introduced into the scheme of things for the first time). So she emptied the bucket and put odd bits in the wastepaper basket.

Then she bit hard on the tire of a car. She tried to put a wheel on the car: "Dr. Winnicott, help!" We got both the wheels on. She wondered now how to fit in some ships.

> *Me:* To fit them in when daddy and mummy are together?
> *Piggle:* Too big. Baby gets too big now.

This was interrupted by someone outside the open window, and then the noise of a plane. Piggle showed anxiety at being distracted by outside noises, but the open window was a real factor, being unusual, and making the outside difficult to exclude. It was very hot.

All this was vague and not clearly articulated. *I let this be so.* Now Piggle seemed to come to the business of the day. She twiddled her perfectly straight hair and said: "My hair's curly."[1] I used this for an interpretation.

Symbolism of curl in hair, a baby

> *Me:* You are wanting a baby of your own.
> *Piggle:* But I've got a girlie-girlie baby.
> *Me:* No, not the Sush Baba.
> *Piggle:* A baby to keep in my bed.
> *Me:* In your curls?
> *Piggle:* Yes.

Play was resumed, and she took two ships and put one on her shoe round her foot. She wanted to go to daddy to show him the two boats.

---

[1] Mother's note: It is Susan who has very curly hair, so that everyone makes a fuss about her.

Piggle: Who loves daddy? The babacar and
      mummy.

    She went and showed daddy the two boats,
and closed the door.

Piggle: I'll be back in half a minute. Help me
      to shut the door. [It was really difficult
      and needed adjusting.]

    She left the keyhole open. She was "eating"
the two boats. I said: "Eating to make babies."
She put all the toys away and fetched daddy.
Then she said: "And then we'll go." The toys
got all sorted out and put away. I interpreted:
"You were frightened to find you wanted to
make babies by eating the ships."

Piggle: Shall I say "hullo" to daddy? [She went
      and came back.] I'll not come back
      again.

    I could hear her father coaxing her to
come back, and she was running to and fro.
Daddy came in and sat in the chair while he and
I had a short talk, because he needed this. Then
both went home.
    I made a note at the end of this hour that
although the notes are ragged and incomplete
(partly due to the hot weather and my sleepiness) the clear point of the hour was her having
her own baby, made by eating. This was the
work she came to do.

COMMENTS

1. Hot weather, and the consequence.

2. The curly hair remark and my interpretation. This seemed to be the important business of the day's work. Her own pregnancy in pregenital fantasy.

3. Making babies by eating—anxieties associated with this.

4. Progression (maturational) from mummy's breasts to daddy's penis.

5. Mrs. Winnicott in the scheme of things.

LETTER FROM THE MOTHER

"Since the Piggle's visit to you the age-old rigamarole every night about the black mummy has virtually stopped and she does not seem frightened of going to sleep.

"On one occasion she again talked about the black mummy saying, 'Take me to Dr. Winnicott, he will help me.' Trying to discourage this just then, I said, 'But he has helped you.' 'Yes, but I tidied the black mummy away.' I just said 'hmm.' Then there was something more about turning over a wastepaper basket, and a dream about feelings. You may know what this is about.

"Twice she very urgently asked to suck my breasts, and she seemed very specially to enjoy the occasion. She got the possessives 'my' and 'your' mixed up when she talked about them.

"After a row about her ill-treatment of her

little sister, she kissed her father and sister, and then said to father: 'Don't kiss me, you make me black. What *is* black, daddy?'

"My husband did not know for certain what you thought about the Piggle, and as she was there at the time of his discussion at the end of the hour he could not speak freely.

"When you told him you found her 'normal' with you, but also raised the subject of an analysis with an analyst I was not sure whether you thought that an analysis was needed, and you could not get things in motion on a deep enough level in the number of interviews you could give the Piggle, and therefore suggested this doctor, or whether you did not think there was a need for anything further unless we were exceedingly anxious.[2]

"I have a sort of prejudice in favor of leaving things to grow their own way, and not to interfere, unless really necessary.

"She still gets these sudden (what seems like) depressions, when she curls up and sucks her thumb, or sits and shouts gibberish, and cannot do anything with herself. In other ways she seems much better, and more alive, but I cannot assess whether she has a chance to regain the depths that she seemed to lose when her baby sister was born. There seemed such a sud-

---

[2] An analyst in supervision with me had asked for a three-year-old child just at this time, and I thought of referring Gabrielle to him. This warped me, made me feel guilty, and so I became muddled when I raised the issue with her father. However, in my considered opinion the fact that the sessions were "on demand" did not alter the fact that the child was having an analysis. D.W.W.

den, agonizing break, and she seemed to grow
up very fast, and somehow spuriously. I wonder
whether she can, without further help, find
what she left behind. She may be doing this
now, but I would not be able to judge. Or
maybe it can never be done, whatever happens.

LETTER TO THE MOTHER

"Thank you for your letter. I am replying
because I know that I said things in rather a
muddled way to your husband. The fact is that
I got twinges of conscience, and I had to make
certain that it was not I who was keeping you
from having a full-scale analysis for the Piggle.
If it were just as easy for you to live in London as
where you are, I think you would probably want
this, that is to say if someone good should be
available. But I am sure that it would not be
easy for you to come and live in London, and a
lot of traveling would be too much of a complication. It is much better to think in terms of
natural recovery, with an occasional visit to me
helping things along a bit.

"The Piggle is a very interesting child, as
you know. You might prefer that she were not
so interesting, but there she is, and I expect that
she will settle down into being quite ordinary
soon. I think a great number of children have
these thoughts and worries, but they are usually
not so well verbalized, and this in Piggle's case
has a lot to do with your both being rather

particularly conscious of childhood matters and tolerant of childhood questions.

"I am full of admiration for the way the Piggle's father has tolerated sitting there with the Piggle using him, when a great deal of what is happening must be a mystery to him.

FROM A PHONE CALL BY THE MOTHER

"The Piggle was better for a while, but then she became depressed and listless again, not sleeping at night, and preoccupied with the concept, dead. She had a dream: 'No seeds came up, or only a little because of bad things inside.' "

Depressive anxieties

LATER COMMENT BY THE MOTHER

"Does this death theme also link up with the part of herself that has to be 'tidied away,' i.e. made dead? The rapacious, envious part, for example?

"I am interested in how many times she tidies Dr. Winnicott away by having him in one room and going out into the other, the waiting room, and shutting the door.[3]

---

[3] To be able to forget has its uses. D.W.W.

SIXTH CONSULTATION
(July 7, 1964)

The patient was now two years and ten months old. I greeted her on the doorstep with: "Hullo Gabrielle." This time I knew I must say Gabrielle, not Piggle. She went to the toys immediately.

Me: Gabrielle has come to see me again.
Gabrielle: Yes.

She put the two big soft animals together and said: "They are together and are fond of each other." She was also joining two carriages of a train.

Me: And they are making babies.
Gabrielle: No, they are making friends.

Concept of ego related-ness

She was still joining up bits of trains and I said: "You could be joining up all the different times that you have seen me." Her reply: "Yes."

Obviously, there are many interpretations to do with the joining of parts of trains, and one can use this according to the way one feels is most appropriate at the moment, or to convey one's own feelings. I reminded Gabrielle of my interpretation of last time about the curly hair having to do with Piggle having a baby of her own.

Gabrielle: Things I think about.

She then made a distinction (in some way or other, quite clearly) between *telling* and *showing* (reminding me of the song in My Fair Lady, "Show Me!").

> *Me:* You mean showing me is better than telling me about something.

Gabrielle took a little bottle and made a noise like the noise of water: "They make a big circle when you make a big splash." She was lisping, and sometimes it was difficult to make out what she said: "I've got a little paddly pool outside" (meaning in the garden) "and two greenhouses. There's our big house, and then my small house."

> *Me:* The small one is yourself.
>
> *Gabrielle:* Just you. [She said this three times and then:] Just Gabrielle. Just Winnicott.

She linked two carriages together.

> *Me:* Gabrielle and Winnicott make friends, but still Gabrielle is Gabrielle and Winnicott is Winnicott.
>
> *Gabrielle:* We can't find our cat, but I saw one

going for a walk. I saw one running
round everything. What pulled this
along?

I helped her, and she said: "Winnicott
catching hold hands."

There was a kind of establishment of
identities here. I said something about Gabrielle and her several relationships with Winnicott, daddy, mummy, and the Sush Baba.
Gabrielle made a Gabrielle noise and said:
"The Sush Baby makes a wa noise," and
another which she did with her hand across her
mouth.

*She was
dealing with
the border-
line between
merging and
separateness*

She was amused at this variety entertain-
ment, using her hand on and off her mouth.
She had blown a fart just before, and I said:
"Perhaps that was a Gabrielle noise." She then
spoke in a recognizable, characteristic manner,
and I said: "This has to do with daddy." There
had been other times when she has spoken in
this special way when strongly identified with
her father.

Gabrielle: Don't talk that way [but we talked
about daddy]. The Sush Baby isn't
old enough to talk. What's this funny
thing?

She held up a handle which was tied to
some string. She wanted me to put it on the
engine so that she could pull it around the
room. She was pleased about this. I said something about its being a baby Gabrielle that she

was remembering, and she said: "No, it's a little sister," then, suddenly, "Look at this lovely picture" (a portrait of a very serious girl of six or seven, rather old-fashioned, that I keep in my room). "It's a girl older than me. She is older than me like I am older than the Sush Baby. She [Susan] can walk without holding anything now." (She demonstrated walking and running and walking and then falling down.) "And she can get up" (also demonstrated).

Conscious leaning on the operation of the maturational processes

> *Me:* So she doesn't need her mummy all the time now.
>
> *Gabrielle:* No. Soon she will grow bigger and do without mummy or daddy, and Gabrielle will be able to do without Winnicott or without anybody at all. Someone will say: "What are you doing?" That's my place. I want to go to your place. Get out of the way.

She was illustrating a King of the Castle game[1] with Gabrielle establishing her own identity and expecting it to be challenged. She now took two carriages and rubbed them together wheel to wheel.

> *Me:* Are they making babies?
>
> *Gabrielle:* Yes. Sometimes I lie on my back with my legs up when the sun is out. Not making babies. I've got a sundress and white knickers.

---

[1] Winnicott, D. W. (1966), Psycho-somatic Illness in its Positive and Negative Aspects. *Internat. J. Psycho-Anal.*, 47:510-516.

She demonstrated lying on her back with her legs up in the air getting the sun.

Gabrielle: I've got new shoes. [Not the ones she was wearing at the time.]

She was undoing one of her shoes and pulling her socks off. There was an "on-off, on-off" activity. She wanted me to look at it, her sock, putting her big fat heel to the hole.

> *Me:* You are showing me big breasts.
Gabrielle: Like feet.

She undid the other shoe, and showed the other heel-pad. She made fun of all this as if one of her feet had gone, in some game she devised.

Gabrielle: It's all on the wrong foot [this was a joke].

She had changed her socks, and so she went to the toys in the bucket. I said: "Gabrielle eats up all the world and so she eats too much" (but at the time the bucket was not over-full). Gabrielle replied: "She doesn't be sick."

She had one shoe off and played at leaving out the sock. There was a complexity here to do with socks and shoes, and she persevered in a very skilled way, but did not succeed.

> *Me:* Isn't it difficult!
Gabrielle: Yes it is.
> *Me:* Gabrielle can't quite do without mummy and she can't quite be a mummy.

So she came to a large train, and she said: "I
hope we didn't come too early." Then she
talked about the reasons why she and her father
were early. They had actually been around the
shops so as not to be too early.

I felt I was now needed to help with a difficult shoestrap, and this was allowed; also the
other one.

Gabrielle: I hear a big bang [actual].
    Me: Is someone cross?
Gabrielle: No. The Sush Baby bangs.

*Identities
becoming
clarified*

Then she whispered that she would go and
see her daddy, and she opened the door quietly
and shut it again. In a minute she was back, her
own self, not needing daddy. She was putting
the toys away.

Gabrielle: The toys are all untidy. What will
        you say?
    Me: Who?
Gabrielle: Dr. Winnicott.

She put the big soft animals (dogs) away.
The tidying process had been in great detail
with sorting out of types of toys.

Gabrielle: Oh, the top came off; never mind;
        mummy's at home.

Then Gabrielle put everything away
neatly, and said: "You have a nice place for toys
haven't you!" (Actually the muddle of my toys
has a place on the floor under a bookcase.) She
found one or two odd toys that had been left out

and put them away: "I keep mine outside in the wastepaper basket."

She was now going out the door, and there was no toy left around. She was some time out with her father in the waiting room, telling him what she had done, and he was talking about it. Then she was getting her father in. She said to him: "I want you to go inside," but he was holding back. He said: "You go in to Dr. Winnicott."

We had now had three quarters of an hour, and I was ready to stop. Father said: "No, no, you go in to Dr. Winnicott."

Gabrielle: No! No! No!
    Me: Come, because it's nearly time to go. Come inside.

She came in and was very friendly.

She asked me whether I was going to have a holiday and what I would do. I said I would go to the country and enjoy myself. That was the end of the session and as she left she said: "When shall I come back?" I replied: "In October."

An important detail in this session was the moment of identity establishment, the King of the Castle game, following the experiments with separateness out of merging.

COMMENTS

1. My knowing she must be greeted as Gabrielle.

2. Gradual development of identity theme.

3. A version of King of Castle statement.

4. Play at *part objects* leading to the idea of breasts (on-and-off games).

5. Greed turning into appetite.

6. Mess into tidiness. Adumbration of mess theme to come.

LETTER FROM THE MOTHER

"She sleeps well at night again. Her only comment on the session was: 'I wanted to tell Dr. Winnicott that my name is Gabrielle, but he knew it already.' This was said with satisfaction."[2]

LETTER FROM BOTH PARENTS, WRITTEN BY MOTHER[3]

"I do not know why I have found it difficult to write to you; perhaps I have been rather mixed up with Gabrielle and not quite separated out, but I hope that this is resolving itself.

"Gabrielle seems to have been very much better, by which I mean that she has been able to invest the outside world with meanings of her own, and has been able to make use of and enjoy whatever opportunities she has had.

---

[2] This detail shows how important it was that I caught her first message, on the doorstep, and I knew I must say Gabrielle and not Piggle, or a name that might have to do with one or another of her many roles. D. W. W.

[3] Telephone conversations not reported here.

"She is not so shy, but she finds it very diffi-cult to make contact with other children, though she longs to do so very much, and suffers from rebuffs. She suffers very much from dis-illusionment, because she pins a lot of hopes on such contacts.

"She gets on remarkably well with her sister, despite some lightning attacks — such as knocking her flat in the middle of the street, announcing that she was tired of having a little sister. Apart from such occasions, she treats her as a person, with a compassionate understand-ing that is most impressive.

"There is still quite a bit of what seems to me somewhat spurious fantasy: I do not know how far she is taken in by it herself, and how far it is a legitimate and effective defense against somewhat inquisitive parents.[4]

"Only these last few days she has again been unable to go to sleep, has been again visited by the black mummy, and has been talking more about going to Dr. Winnicott. She seems very preoccupied with being poisoned; and she ate a berry that she insisted was poison-ous, telling us how ill she was going to be. She also insists that her 'brrr' is stuck inside her, though she does not seem to suffer from physi-cal constipation. But all this has not been manifest for the rest of the summer. It meant a lot to her to have your telephone number.

[4] Could this join up with my being kept ignorant with respect to the black phenomena? D. W. W.

"You seem to have made so very much difference to her, and set things in motion again when they seemed to have rammed themselves into a most debilitating vicious circle. She even seems to look more like the solid little girl she was before Susan was born, and somehow continuity appears to have been re-established."

LETTER TO THE PARENTS FROM MYSELF

"I received the postcard from Gabrielle. I think you would like me to see her again, and I will keep a time for her. You may feel, however, that it would be a good idea to leave things for a few weeks, in which case I hope you will let me know.

"From what I have seen of Gabrielle, and from your letter, I do feel that we must not just think of her in terms of illness. There is much that is healthy in her. Perhaps you would let me know what you want me to do."

(I have to remember here my bias belonging to the fact that I had no vacancy for a new treatment case; but also I did feel that these parents had some special reason for not relying on the developmental process which in this child might see her through apart from the provision of a treatment.)

LETTER FROM THE PARENTS

"Thank you for your letter and the offer of an appointment, which we would be pleased to keep.

"We also feel that Gabrielle can no longer be thought of as a very sick little girl; so many more areas of herself seem to have come to life again. And yet there are very marked pockets of distress and anxiety, which sometimes seem to lead to her cutting off all feeling altogether— and so living a very articulate, but two-dimensional life.

"When we last wrote to you, she was just beginning to have difficulties in going to sleep again, after having been quite all right during most of the summer; and she is now up regularly for about three to four hours after bedtime.

"She now has a 'Nice black mummy,' who cuts her nails (you may remember how she used to scratch her face at night when in distress, and she has done this lately). The black mummy, however, came to cut off her thumb with a carving knife. But she said that she would tell Dr. Winnicott that the black mummy had gone.

"At the moment she is extremely concerned about her parents dying; but she talks of this in a very feelingless, blank sort of way. To her mummy: 'I'd like you to be dead.'—'Yes. You would also be sorry.'—'Yes. I'll keep your photo in my suitcase.'

"She gives hints of the most disgusting things happening between her parents, and was deeply shocked and upset when she saw more than usual of her mother when changing for a bath. Though these seem fairly usual preoccupations, her distress and subsequent cutting off

of feeling, and worry about them at night, seem
to us to indicate that a little help may still be
needed.

"We took her to a nursery play group
where, as we told you, she finds it difficult to
make any contact, though she seems to want to:
'Mummy, take a book. I'll be bored, and then I
won't know what to do, and then I won't know
anyone, and then I won't want anyone to look at
me.' "

SEVENTH CONSULTATION
(October 10, 1964)

Gabrielle (now three years, one month) came with her father and went straight to the toys, her head touching my elbow as I was sitting on the floor. She took a big soft toy.

Gabrielle. Shall I start with the houses in a row? Did you hear my bell? I rang three times. Mr. Winnicott[1] what's this?

Me: It's a truck.

Gabrielle: Oh [and she started joining it up with something]. All the troubles have gone so I have nothing left to tell you.

Me: I am seeing Gabrielle without any troubles, just Gabrielle.

Gabrielle: I had a black mummy that troubled me but she has gone away now. I didn't like the mummy and she didn't like me. She talked nonsense to me.

---

[1] Here starts a recurrent indication of a nontherapist Winnicott.

She had arranged a long row of houses put together in a rather straight S-shaped curve, with a church at each end. Then she took the electric light bulb with the face on it and said: "I forgot this." There was something here about being angry at the baby being born. She said: "A little girl is going into the church with the big girl." There was some play here which is not recorded properly. It had to do with putting something in for the dogs and the cattle — and something disturbed the houses at each end of the S-shaped bend.

Gabrielle: Now we will make a railway.

She took two stones she had brought with her previously in a paper bag, and there was a bigger stone in the bag. It had something to do with the black mummy. Then she brought the big stone into relation with the two smaller ones.

Gabrielle: Mr. Winnicott why don't you have more trains?

She looked for some more and found them, although of course she knew about them: "How did they come to you Mr. Winnicott?"

There were cars and a road and another stone; she swept them all away and said: "This train pulls both the trains; now . . . more boats, trains" (lots of noises, talking to herself in an unintelligible way).

After a time she dealt with this by looking at me and smiling with the intention of getting

Here she was holding a personal inner reality experience, only vaguely letting me know about the details of content

a response. Presumably this was related to *the obscurity of what was going on because of her withdrawn state* and of her playing in a way which was not intelligible to me. Somewhere here she put a train on a ship, which was absurd in one sense because the toy train was so much bigger than the toy ship.

Query: protest about holiday

Gabrielle: Do you like my toys? I do, they are like French toys aren't they? We have been to France. I didn't want anybody to be in France with me.

Reference to withdrawn state

Here she was playing with the very small wooden train, and she took bits of wood and arranged them radially enumerating them one, two, three. She was pushing a stick down into the carpet trying to make it stand, but it wouldn't stand. I helped a little and I followed the train along. She almost threw the tractor coupled with the wagon at me because she didn't want it. She now made a very deliberate toy arrangement. There was a central S-shaped line of houses with a church at each end, and on her side there was herself and many objects representing herself. On the other side, i.e., on my side of the S-shaped line, was the tractor she had thrown at me and also myself and other objects. This was a not-me representation. It was an absolutely deliberate communication showing she had achieved this separation from me as part of the establishment of herself. It was also a defense against being reinvaded. There was something that crossed the line. It had to do

Aggressive act, putting her aggressive impulses out, and into me

with some cars that came from her side to mine, and she said something about "nobody knows how. . . ."

Eventually she evidently felt that something had happened, because she started singing, and when I said something about her having inside things she completed the sentence by saying that they were kept "tucked away" (I made a special note that this was her own expression). She was talking to herself: "A little boy had to be put with a little girl to go with the little girl; Richard my friend; and Sarah" (and some other girls' names). There were now two lines formed by houses and other toys which met at one end. One of the girls was called Clare.[2] I think this had to do with the summer holiday. She was telling me about a place where Clare lived.

Gabrielle: That is where I go sometines. No I don't.

She conveyed to me that there were mumps there at present, which made her unable to go there.

Gabrielle: So I can't go to them any more although I want to go. I could not see them and they could not come to see me. I don't know what to do. So I went to school to play. I liked it. Everything was the wrong way round because of mumps. They can't go out or bathe. They want to but their

Quarantine theme is the same as the defensive boundary between me and not-me

[2] Pure *chance* that Clare is Mrs. Winnicott's name!

mumps won't let them. Mummy's worried that I'll get a cold from her. So mummy said "no," then she did ask, I was terribly . . . I don't know what to do.

Me: I don't understand [I had interpreted in terms of the establishment of identities].

Gabrielle: Now where's that pretty boat? Where did I put the boats? [We looked but couldn't find them.] Could they be in the bucket? No they couldn't. Look at my dirty hand. [She had the boats in her hand.] But where are the others? I wonder where they have gone. Here's another. I used to know where the boats were. I used to be used to you but now I am not. I am grown up. They walk and talk.

There was something about a peacock.

Peacock =
D.W.W.

Gabrielle: But they don't understand. It's baa. The peacocks just shake their heads like saying no. They never say "Oh dear."

Gabrielle sang a song to illustrate the use of "Oh dear." She then arranged a whole series of boats pointing away from herself: "Who go in all these boats?" Here she was singing a song that had to do with boats. She arranged boats again and I arranged bits of wood: "We both made boats. Now we will tidy away. Why are you having so many boats for me? It's funny."

She went on with the play in which there were many boats in front of her pointing away from her. There was a similar row of cars further away, and a lot of other things on her side of the line separating her from the tractor and me. All the arrangements on her side of the line were carefully put so that they did not touch each other. She was singing, about having cars of various colors.

Defense: disparate internal objects between living and dead, controlled

Gabrielle: What is this string for? Let's put it here.

I had to cut it off so that it was just right, and she pulled along the engine right across the length of the room.

Gabrielle: Where have the scissors gone to? [because I used a knife].
   Me: I have left my scissors upstairs [I always have scissors in my pocket].

She went back to the toys.

   Me: You are ready to go again [because I saw that she was tidying up].
Gabrielle: Where do the houses go [and so on].

She gave me a train and started throwing things across to me because, after all, I was on the other side of the border of the barrier. "There you are," she said many times, "there." She now conveyed in the play the idea of me in a box. She also gave me something to keep, something she liked.

D.W.W. over there

Gabrielle: When I come again I shall find you
have tidied everything up.

She seemed to be free from something, so
that I made a note, "Free at last." It was something to do with the babacar. She said: "Wait a
minute. Now I'll clear everything. There we
are." She put away the cars very carefully: "I
don't want to spoil them." She counted the
trains: "Which is best for the trains?" And she
put them lying down all nice and tidy: "Get the
toys tidy." Then she came to the stones: "Now
put away mummy. Now where does this go, Mr.
Winnicott?" And she went on: "Tidy away
nicely." She played some with the Optrex eyebath, then: "Who put the dark thing in the
toys?" She seemed to be nearly finished, and she
fetched the string bundle and put it in the
bucket. There was a box full of all the oddments: "There we are. Now where does this go?
Now it's a bit tidy." There was one box left. She
placed it just so: "Now. Tidy the mat now.
What a nice material this carpet is! Who gave it
to you? The hard carpet [haircord, under the
'nice' oriental mat] isn't so very nice. It's just to
make the floor safe. Awfully nice material this
mat. And this one too [going over to the chair]
and this." She went over to the couch and examined the materials of the couch and the
cushions. She went further and said: "and this
chair's awfully nice"; and then she went to
daddy to take him home.

Anxiety managed by superego establishment and acceptance

Observation of external objects, Objectivity

COMMENTS

1. Herself as herself, not because of troubles.
2. Clear statement of me and not-me.
3. Intercommunication experiments.
4. Quarantine. Defensive wall between me and not-me.
5. Control of external objects in tidying.
6. Objectivity *re* external objects.

Positive transference was now in part to an actual (i.e., not therapeutic) Mr. Winnicott and his room (wife).

One can expect the black phenomena also to become aspects of objects in the actual world external to herself, and separate from her.

Persecutory black belongs to the residues of merging regressively, in organized defense.

LETTER FROM THE PARENTS

"Gabrielle would like to see you again, I believe fairly urgently though she is hesitant about asking. She suggested I should send you a present. She also wanted to send a present to a woman who used to work for us, of whom she was very fond, and who left us.[3]

"The theme of the black mummy has been cropping up again, though in a different way: 'I haven't written to the black mummy . . . She gave me a lovely vase with something in it that

---

[3] Gratitude implies acceptance of separateness, of the reality principle, a fruit of disillusionment. D.W.W.

grows.' ('The Wattie,' our daily help, an elderly woman loved by us all, has given her a bulb in a glass jar.) 'I am frightened of the black mummy. I haven't paid her. She gave me a lovely wooden cup.' Paying the black mummy has been mentioned repeatedly.

"Quite recently she has started to have difficulties in going to sleep again. She needs to have all her dolls, teddies, and books on the bed, so there is hardly room for her. In the daytime, she has of late tended to behave badly, as if our authority and ourselves counted for nothing. Perhaps we have been a bit remiss about being firm and asserting ourselves, and we are trying to remedy this. But, on the occasions that Gabrielle is well, she is very well indeed.[4]

[4] Difficulty in management of ill child who is recovering: the question, when to be firm and act on the basis of child's being normal? i.e., recovery from pathological superego toward being a spontaneous child in a family setting. D.W.W.

EIGHTH CONSULTATION
(December 1, 1964)

Gabrielle (now three years, three months) came in and said: "I'll play with these toys first, then with this nice little toy." She had brought a great big plastic soldier—"Nice. Let's get them all on the nice village."

Theme of denial of nastiness

I said something about the existence of nastiness too. She took the tractor and said: "That's nice. Susan got a dog too." She got some string and said the tractor could be fixed onto the little train. "We went in the train," and she put the train behind us (this was being funny and there were other indications that there might be something anal in the material). "Lots of trains you have got Mr. Winnicott." She wanted me to help her fix the string.

Gabrielle: This is nice. I could have come here in the afternoon, couldn't I? That would be nice. Just to visit you [she was putting more trains behind the other trains]. Don't push them away, train.

99

Me: Where do the Winnicott trains live, here or inside Gabrielle?

Gabrielle: Inside there [she pointed]. What goes on in this train? And this one? [she found a hook belonging to a carriage]. When I put a train—ha! ha! ha! I nearly squashed the soldier and made him cry. He comes from my home. Oh this is a nice train behind there. Where is the station Mr. Winnicott? [I put up two fences.] Yes, that's the station" [she was joining together carriages]. This is the railway station. I get help from Mr. Winnicott. What's that?

Me: For luggage and things.

Gabrielle: Here's another old train with a big engine. I have got nice new shoes. This is a truck for luggage. It had better go on this [and she was arranging the trucks and the luggage]. Susan is a great nuisance. Jigsaw. She comes near and disturbs it. I pushed her away a lot of times and she came near. She is a nuisance. When she is a bigger Susan she will be able to do what I do; she keeps coming and disturbing me. I would like a new baby who doesn't come near and take things away.

I said something about making her black.

Gabrielle: No it makes her cry. Then I shout

loud, I get very cross and I shout
louder, and she cries again, and then
mummy and daddy are cross. She is
like Kiko, that is a wild bear in
France. Once they both started a bear
like Kiko. There was a fond mummy
Kiko and baby was outside the cage
and she was in the cage. She was enor-
mous like a baby inside a mummy.
Baby Kiko didn't stay in the cage.
Monkeys do and lions and bears.

Me: What else?

Gabrielle: Not cows or giraffes. Snakes do. Dogs
do, I think so, no. Cats too. We got a
black cat. It comes every night to see
me. I go to the flat. There is the
black cat. I stroke him. Sometimes
he is in my house. Mummy gives him
something to eat. What's this for? [It
was a crooked end to a house.] Why
is it like that? It was made by crooked
wood.

Me: Made by a crooked man [thinking of
the nursery rhyme and carrying the
idea backwards].

Here she was eating the plastic man. I said
she was eating the man because she wanted to
eat me.

Me: If you eat me that would be taking
me away inside you, and then you
would not mind going.

Gabrielle: Where does he sit? He could go in the

> little house. Not the crooked one,
> this one [a church] or this one. It is
> an especially nice one.

She sat back on the lamb. She kept looking
at the soldier by the train.

Gabrielle: This is a silly dog [the lamb]. Who
tied a ribbon round his neck? It's
pretty. I can tie that too, but the
baby can't. Susan not able to. Sometimes I tie a little dress round my
baby to make it look pretty. And
then I got out shopping with it. Oh,
who did this? [the other soft toy, the
faun]. They don't stand. Yes they do.
Nice dogs.

She was balancing them, and between us
we were barking and saying woof-woof. I said
something about her and the Sush Baby.

Gabrielle: Do you know Susan was cross [and
she made cross noises], she really is
cross and she cries. When I am a bit
cross I cry a bit. I cry at night with
my fingers in my mouth. I have to
cry with my mouth open. What does
this belong to? Maybe a little wheel
off a little car. This bucket should be
here. These are nice houses. I am
making a little house for the dog. All
the houses are for the dogs. They
quarrel in the house. Another dog
comes in. Here's another house [it
was a separate house].

I talked about her and Susan needing separate rooms or separate houses because they quarrel.

Gabrielle: When I am big I will get old before Mummy's old, before she is old. What is this for? [She once more took the blue eye-bath and examined it.] If mummy got old I would get old too. Make it into a little house. Say: all the dogs come [that is to say, each has a house] so they don't quarrel. They usually quarrel, bark, awful noise ... I think Daddy wants me to go.

Me: But have you got rid of your fears?

Gabrielle: I'm scared of the black Susan; so I play with your toys. I hate Susan. Yes I hate her very much only when she takes my toys away [implied: here in Dr. W.'s house she has use of toys *and Susan is excluded*]. This is such a pretty house. When Susan's dressed nicely, she's so pretty. Then she would love this house and do you know what she does? When she loves me she comes and bends down and says aaa and kisses me. When Mummy's ready to go into the town, it's nice of her, when Susan loves me.

Me: You hate and love Susan, both at the same time.

Gabrielle: When we play with mud we are both

Anxiety content: probably hate of sister

Ambivalence held

black. We both bathe, we both   *Mud is feces,*
change our clothes. Then Mummy   *i.e., fused love*
sometimes thinks she's muddy and
Susan too. I like Susan. Daddy likes
Mummy. Mummy likes Susan best.
Daddy likes me best. Shall I go out
and tell Daddy about not wanting to
go yet? I can't open the door; oh I
got it.

She went out to Daddy (40 minutes from
start). She came back: "Mr. Winnicott what's
the time?" I told her. "Five minutes more. Bang
the door!" (she did). "Which way round does it
go? I've lots of clothes on" (enumerated all details). "I'm much too warm. Like . . ." (she
repeated this many times). "Susan takes her
dress off when she wants to take it off [she took
the string]. We could put this on the train.
When we like to play we play ring-a-ring-a-
roses. You fix it" (I do). "We could cut this off.
Cut it off! [I do]. Thank you, Mr. Winnicott."

She was playing with the train and the
string: "That's better, it's too small. I have to
bend down a bit." She told me about the actual
train she came in. It had to be moved by some
very very strong string.

Gabrielle: Please play. . . . [There was a cart for
some soldiers]. Susan sometimes pulls
things upside down. I don't get cross
about it [pulls the train away]. Oh
. . . would you like me to tidy the
things away? [Hint obvious.]

Me: Leave it to me.

Gabrielle went off with her father, *leaving me with the mess and muddle.* Compare this with her previous careful tidying up and denial of muddle. Gabrielle showed growing confidence now in my ability to tolerate muddle, dirt, inside things, and incontinence and madness.

COMMENTS

1. The key word was nice, presage of nastiness. Nastiness = fusion of aggressive expulsion with loving giving = dependence on how it is received.

2. The beginnings of dealing with loss by incorporation and its consequence: anxiety and support about internal objects. Defense: decoration of outside of self (ribbon-neck).

3. Letting loose of some internal objects from disparateness (defense — see previous sessions.)

4. Ambivalence and mud.

5. First time leaving me the muddle.

LETTER FROM THE FATHER

"On the way home Gabrielle was for much of the time a 'little baba'; her thumb was rammed in her mouth, and she would only talk 'b-ba' (she sucks her thumb a great deal now, having started this only when Susan was born).

"When she arrived home she wanted to see Susan, and was almost in tears when she was asleep. Then she insisted on doing a jigsaw puzzle before she settled down to her lunch; it seemed to mean a lot to her to fit it together.

"This morning she woke up shivering, as she had dreamed about the black Susan. The black Susan 'wanted to make me tired, to keep me awake by crying.' "

LETTER FROM THE PARENTS

"Just a note before you see Gabrielle.

"A few days ago she said, and has repeated once or twice since, 'I have paid the black mummy.'

"Paid" means: "I left mud, feces, muddle, which was accepted"

"[Mother's note:] 'Paying the black mummy' has always worried me. I wonder to what extent this wasn't placating, using valuable energies, using part of herself to keep the black mummy quiet, and so not to be made black in return. And I wonder if this sort of thing might lead to rigid defenses against confusion between good and black, or in actual confusion.

"The black mummy has settled down. This has not, however, made her go to sleep any earlier. She is now troubled by the black Susan. She comes to me in the night because she likes me but she is black.

"In reality Susan is very tender with Gabrielle, but very forceful when she wants something. She can be ruthlessly impinging."

LETTER FROM THE MOTHER

"Gabrielle has asked for you several times. She has been remarkably well, but quite lately she has started to worry again at night, and to appear to be not quite herself in the daytime.

"She has kept asking to be called Susan (her sister's name), and not to be called by her own name, and she keeps sucking her thumb and being rather listless and uninterested in things. She called me again in the middle of last night. 'What are you worried about?' — 'Myself, I ought to make myself dead, but I don't want to, because I am so beautiful.'

"She has also talked about wanting me dead and sleeping with her father 'and then I think, "but I want just *this* mummy." '

"She wants to bring Susan to you 'because Dr. Winnicott is a very good maker-better of babies.'

"When she does something such as painting, she gets very quickly discouraged, and then messes up everything. She loves cleaning and making things better."

LETTER TO THE PARENTS FROM DR. WINNICOTT

"It distresses me that I am not able to offer Gabrielle an immediate time. This term is a very difficult one for me. It would be possible for you to tell her that I intend to see her although I cannot see her immediately. Do not hesitate to ring me up or write me if you feel I have forgotten. You can give Gabrielle my love.

LETTER FROM THE PARENTS

"Gabrielle has been asking so urgently to see you, and seems to have been so depressed of late, that we thought we would let you know.

"The other evening she wanted us to look up the night trains to London to come and see you 'because I can't wait any more.'

"She is increasingly unwilling to go to sleep. One reason she gave was that she did not want to grow, so as not to grow up and have babies (this is a change in attitude—she used to want babies previously). More recently, though, she does not want to sleep, because 'I want to feel alive.'

"She sucks her thumb constantly, and seems generally sad and strained. She has been waking up very early in the morning, and at night, with 'black mummy' worries.

"We had to promise Gabrielle we would write to you; and also we feel that something must be done to help her. We enclose a painting which Gabrielle urgently wants to send you, done this morning."

LETTER FROM THE PARENTS

"We are very relieved that you are able to find a time for Gabrielle. It seemed to make a great difference to her to be told she was coming to see you. 'Then I can get all my worries out—but there won't be enough time.' She stopped sucking her thumb all that morning.

"We would like to tell you about one special worry we have about Gabrielle, but we don't quite know how to put it. She seems to have difficulties with her identity. She disowns herself, flatly denying that she had bitten Susan on the bottom; or she *is* Susan, refusing to be called by her own name, making puddles on the floor and whining.

"She also has a side of herself that seems so astoundingly mature that it may be that our response to her makes it more difficult for her to bring the different sides together.

"She has a bad cough and a cold. I hope it is all right to bring her."

MOTHER'S NOTE

"It is not at all clear to me why she had such difficulties with her identity and had to be the mummy or Susan, not the Piggle. When she wipes *her* nose, she tells you about *Susan's* cold. And I remembered how even at this time, when she answered to her own name, she would tell people how *Susan* was, when they asked her how *she* was. Does this link up, I wonder, with leaving you early, and 'I put my bad worries into Dr. W. and take good worries in'—or something like that."

NINTH CONSULTATION
(January 29, 1965)

Gabrielle (now three years, four months) went straight into the room and over to the toys, letting her father go to the waiting room.

Gabrielle: I have seen him before several times [as she took one of the soft animals from the general mess of small toys. Taking some trains:] This is something to fit onto the truck; sometimes Susan does get excited in the mornings. I called to the grownups: "Susan is excited!" She says: "My big sister's up." She wakes mummy and daddy in the night; a little monster. Mama! Dada! She has to have a bottle in the night! [Almost giving me Susan instead of herself.]

All this time she was playing with the toys: "This one hasn't anything to fit onto it" (showing me a truck with no hook). "This is all nice...." She took something out of the general muddle. I said: "Eyebath" (it was the blue Optrex eyebath which she always had been interested in). She picked things out of the bucket. She had an awful cold and wanted a tissue, which I got for her. But in her conversation, this was all mixed up with talk about trucks. Wiping her nose, she said: "Susan has a bad cold."

> *Me:* I suppose *I'll* be sneezing tomorrow.
> *Gabrielle:* You'll be sneezing tomorrow. I know, Mr. Winnicott, you fix this onto here.

I pointed out to her that she was trying to make some kind of thing out of a lot of parts, and this meant making one thing out of Susan, Winnicott, mummy, and daddy. These were separate things inside her, but she could not make them join up into one thing. She was now singing while pushing the train, and she got hold of the string which was all caught up round one of the wooden engines. She said something about a bundle, and got me to help her.

Development of concepts about whole objects

> *Gabrielle:* A little bit of string. Put it on. [She was talking to herself]. We have decided Susan is really a little monster. We call her Mrs. Hickabout. Simon and King[1] Kickabout Round and Round the Coal Fire; a little girl

[1] The nursery rhyme: "Old Sir Simon the King
And young Sir Simon the squire
And old Mrs. Hickabout
Kicked Mr. Kickabout
Round about our coal fire."

burning chestnuts. This little girl's taking a long time [apparently a comment from Father about Susan].

About the black mummy. She comes every night. I can't do anything. She's very difficult. She gets on my bed. She is not allowed to touch. "No, this is my bed. I'm going to have it. I've got to sleep in it." Daddy and mummy are in bed in another room. "No, that's *my* bed. No! No! No! That's *my* bed." That's the black mummy. Someone playing the band. Two little Turks [again apparently a comment from someone on the two children]. Daddy may say I'm vile.

Me: What's vile?

Gabrielle: People who are naughty. I'm naughty sometimes. [Here was something about traveling on the train coming up to London.] We went underground. Look! [She caught hold of the soft animal toy.] Susan was sad at Gabrielle going away to London. Oh [sing-song voice] when will my big sister come back? She needs me to help when she uses the potty. This morning I opened the toilet; she came into me; wanted me to take something off to do bolly. I have a great worry every night. It's the black mummy. I want my bed. She hasn't got one. There's no mackintosh so I

must get wet. She takes no care of
her little girls.

Me: You are talking about your mummy
and how she didn't know how to care
for you.

Gabrielle: Mummy does know. It's the mummy
with a black face very horrid.

Me: Do you hate her?

Gabrielle: I don't know what's happening to
me. Goodness I am being forced out
of bed by the black mummy and I've
got such a nice bed. "No, Piggle,
you haven't got a nice bed" [here she
was "in" an experience]. "No, Piggle
you haven't got a nice bed." She is
angry with mummy. "You have got
such a horrid bed for this horrid
girl!" The black mummy likes me.
She thinks I am dead. Horrible
[necessarily obscured]. It's bull [?] to
see me. She doesn't know about
children or babies. The black mummy doesn't know about babies.

Me: Your mummy didn't know about
babies when she had you, but you
taught her to be a good mother to
Susan.

Gabrielle: Susan is terribly sad if I go out
shopping, and she is happy when I
come back. Oh mummy, mummy,
mummy! [she said this with great
sadness]. I don't want a nice big
sister who will kiss when she is sad

*Splitting the
good mother
from the bad
mother*

*Experience
of contact
between self
and good
mummy*

and to go away. You have got toys behind your back. It's difficult to get them out. Here are some houses. Susan woke me up in the night once.

Me: Oh what a nuisance!

(before baby sister came) now lost. Experience of loss, memory of good experience

Gabrielle was joining an engine and some trucks, but with difficulty because they would not fit. There was a long period of indefinite activity here, and I myself may have been somewhat drowsy in this period with nothing definite going on (my notes are deficient here, indicating my own difficulty). She was muttering about trains, something about wheels, and then she said: "I am cold. I had some gloves." My withdrawal here has to be taken into account. It itself was related to the indefinite material because of Gabrielle's withdrawal. In a sense I "took" her projection, or "caught" her mood. Here I made a definite note that I had been sleepy, but I have no doubt whatever I would have come awake if something had been going on. This vague period ended with her telling me to draw a tiger on the yellow electric bulb.

Gabrielle: That's lovely. I have seen this one before. I shall show daddy. For a long time mummy didn't want a baby and then she wanted a boy but she had a girl.[2] We are going to have a boy when we are grown up. Me and

[2] Mother's note: She knew that I did not mind about boy or girl when she was born, and that I wanted a boy when I had had a girl, i.e., when Susan was born.

Susan. We will have to find a daddy
man to marry. Here are some boots.
Did you hear what I said Dr. Winnicott? I got some lovely trucks for
luggage.

I made some interpretations here dealing
with herself in the position of boy relative to
Susan in the oedipal triangle. She went on:
"This is my bed so I can't go by train to Mr.
Winnicott. No you don't want to go to Mr.
Winnicott. He really does know about bad
dreams. No he doesn't. He does. No he doesn't"
(this was a conversation between herself and
another part of herself). "He doesn't want me to
get rid of her."

I talked about the black mummy as a
dream, trying to make it quite clear to Gabrielle
that the black mummy belongs to dreaming,
and that upon waking there are the contrasting
ideas of the black mummy and real people. The
time had come when we could talk about
dreams instead of an inner reality, delusionally
"actual" inside.

Gabrielle: I was lying all still with my gun. I
tried to shoot her. She just went
away. Do you know what people do
to me? I was asleep. I could not talk.
It was only a dream.

Me: Yes it was a dream with the black
mummy in the dream.

I asked whether she wanted the bad mother
to be a real person or a dream person.

Gabrielle: Do you know in TV there are people shooting? [here she "shot" by digging her finger many times into the hole in the belly of the faun]. I wondered why it made such a funny noise. Somebody put straw inside it. She's crying. She's not ready to make babies. Did you get the card I sent you? I didn't mean anything. You know what I have got? I have some dominos for . . . [she named a boy baby in the neighborhood. She was playing with ships]. Somebody shooting and so they can't stand up [she took a green truck]. This is a nice color [she made a musical noise]. Susan sometimes tickles me.

Gabrielle then said something like "Gag-gaagur." This had to do with the conversation between herself and Susan: "What is this?" (It was part of the fence.) "Mr. Winnicott, I can't stay here for quite a lot longer, so could you see me another day?"

Anxiety relative to theme not yet clear

It would be easy to think that she was dissatisfied with me because of my having been sleepy, but in fact it is likely that the whole episode (even including my sleepiness) had to do with Gabrielle's great anxiety, making clear communication impossible. *Anxiety had certainly to do with the black mummy dream.* I asked here about dreams and she said: "I dreamed she was dead. She wasn't there." At this point she did something which I am sure had great significance, whatever it symbolized. I could tell this from the fact that the whole quality of the session altered. It was as if everything else had been held back for this to happen. She took the blue eyebath and put it in and out of her mouth, making sucking noises, and it could be said that she experienced something very near to a generalized orgasm.

This is the significant thing in the child's whole behavioral experience with the analytic setting

Gabrielle: I loved her very much. Baah. This is nice. Who shot mummy? Teddy had a gun and it's broken. The black mummy is my bad mummy. *I liked the black mummy* [this was a dream being reported in play form. She went on talking about the lovely truck:] Let's play on.

Black now becomes the negation of the luminous or white or idealized mummy of the preambivalent era, of the mother as a subjective object

This was when I said it was time to go. In other words, anxiety had been overcome in some way during the hour—a new stage in the achieving of ambivalence.

In the evening the parents rang me up to ask for any report I might want to make, and I said that the hour had been a difficult one to understand but that everything led up to the place where mummy was shot dead. In this setting the black mother is the good mother who has been lost. The incident with the eyebath and the orgastic experience seemed to be a place where Gabrielle discovered the lost good mother along with her own orgastic capacity which evidently was lost with the good mother.

NOTE

There is now a recollection of an actual mother, orgiastically eaten and also shot in ambivalence, replacing the more primitive split into good mother and black mother related to each other because of the split between the subjective and that which is objectively perceived.

A few days later the parents rang to report a very great change in the child. She had become "a richer person and a wholehearted child." She was now playing with her little sister and she was less persecuted. This had the result that the little sister was not attacking her so much. She had become affectionate with her mother and was able to play with her much more than previously. She said spontaneously: "I put out my bad worries on to Dr. Winnicott and took in good ones" (cashing in on the new separation of identities).

This improvement lasted for three weeks. Then the child began to worry again about the black mummy. During these three weeks there had been so much improvement that the parents had felt encouraged. The child had become ill physically, but in spite of this she continued to be more lively than she had been, and was playing with her sister. She had been saying: "When is Winnicott's birthday? I want to send him a present, but it mustn't be wrapped up." She once told her mother: "You become a black mummy when you are cross."

Wrapped up would mean obscured by defense mechanisms, as is the meaning of her play when she is withdrawn.

In the deepest layer, however, the black mummy is the original good or subjective mummy.

COMMENTS

(A bad cold.)

1. Trouble with internal objects or objects of her current experience in inner psychic reality terms.

2. Black mummy: rival over beds, concept of being "vile."

3. Black mummy as a split-off version of mother, one that does not understand babies, or one who understands them so well that her absence or loss makes everything black.

4. Positive element in black mummy. Sadness in "mummy, mummy, mummy" = memory.

5. Doldrums area in the interview: mutual.

6. Black mummy now in dream terms: reverie.

7. Memory turning into erotic oral experience with orgastic quality.

8. Death of *beloved* black mummy (shot dead). This is anger with the mummy who was lost: goes with angry incorporation alternative.

9. The present for Dr. W.—not wrapped up—i.e., open, plain, obvious (baby).

LETTER FROM THE PARENTS, WRITTEN BY THE MOTHER

"Gabrielle would like me to write and ask

you to see her. She did not, as so often, give me
any reason, but she seems to consider it urgent.
Her request came on the evening of my birthday; it seemed to pain her greatly that the
birthday was not hers, though she did her
utmost to make it a success; she came over to me
several times to hit me in mock earnest and she
could not sleep, 'because of my birthday.'

"She seemed to us very well since her last
interview with you; she gives the impression of
much greater robustness and definiteness than
formerly.

"The only negative thing I can think of
reporting is her thumb sucking, and the way she *Thumb sucking*
draws attention to herself in grown-up company *link with the*
by shouting gibberish and being generally ex- *orgastic ex-*
cited; with children she is shy. *perience with*
the object

"With her baby sister she is forbearing and
understanding to an extent that sometimes puts
me to shame.

"I feel I have not told you anything really
important this time; her own life is very private,
and lived inside herself.

"(Since this was written Gabrielle has sent
you two drawings which we enclose. The envelope had 'love to Mr. Winnicott' on it.)"

LETTER FROM THE MOTHER

"Gabrielle is by no means back where she
had been. She seems much more all of a piece,
though sometimes this seems to be gained by a
certain grim determination on her part.

"She was very urgent about seeing you. 'How can one bring babies to Dr. Winnicott? I want to bring Susan.' We wonder how far Susan has become part of Gabrielle. She is always talking about Susan, mostly about her boldness and naughtiness, even when people ask her about herself.

"If I were on the lookout for worries about her I would pick on her frequent melancholy thumb sucking, and her outbursts of wanton destructiveness. Unlike her sister, she is never destructive in a casual way; she is meticulously careful of her things, sorting and washing them a lot. Destructiveness seems suddenly to come over her, when she will demolish and tear up things, apparently quite without passion, just with grim determination.

Possessed by split-off unfused aggression

"But she also plays creatively now much more often than she used to."

TENTH CONSULTATION
(March 23, 1965)

Gabrielle (now three years, six months) was brought by her father, and I kept her waiting a little. She had said repeatedly: "Get back to your dollies." She got to work as usual with her and me on the floor, and all the time she was babbling. There was something about: "Susan's book in the train. My favorite book. Natalie Susan, a pretty name. It's Italian. I am Deborah Gabrielle."

She was enjoying the articulation of these names.[1] She was among the toys, and she took up one and said: "What on earth is this? All kinds of things that I haven't...." and she was joining up trucks: "So many toys. Goodness, what a lot of toyees" (I had not added any toys since the first visit, except the Optrex eyebath, as reported).

She was talking to herself and very contented. She went on: "What on earth...?" She

---

[1] Cf. the orgastic mouthing of the object in the last session.

was taking up another train and she was joining
up the carriages.

I made a comment here that she was joining up herself and myself.

Gabrielle: In the train ... apple juice ... we
        had great fun in the train all to-
        gether. There was a long, long train.
        This is long [and there was a wave of
        the arm to describe the length].
   Me: The long distance has to do with the
        time between now and your last visit,
        and Gabrielle is taking a long time to
        find out if I am alive.

This seemed to be some kind of cue for her.

Gabrielle: When will your birthday be? I want
        to give you some presents.

In the setting I found myself ready with the
idea of linking birth and death.

   Me: What about my death day?
Gabrielle: We will see what we can get for you.
        Mummy wrote a letter to France; it
        takes three hours, quite a day to get
        there.
   Me: If I were dead it would take longer
        still.
Gabrielle: You would not open it because you
        would be dead. It's terrible.

Then she said something about its being
like a shot, a string parcel. You put the thing
down and the powder shot out; it's very dangerous; they only die if a snake bites them. She

went on in some way with the theme of death (not accurately recorded).

Gabrielle: It's terrible. Snakes are horrible. But only if one hurts them. Then they bite. Mummy once went to the zoo and there was a parrot there who said: "Hullo darling" [she said this in a very funny way like a parrot].

Me: You mean there were some other things in the zoo, like snakes.

Gabrielle: I said to my daddy: "Are these poisonous?" I was just going to put my hand to stroke it, but daddy pulled me away [there was something here about a little girl]: You could tell she was happy by her face.

Me: Are you a happy little girl?

Gabrielle said something about Susan.

Gabrielle: I want to destroy if I build anything. But she doesn't want to do that. She had bottles with a teat. First I started feeding her, but she walked away and didn't let me. She's a nice little baba.

Me: Sometimes you shoot her.

Gabrielle: No, sometimes I am at peace with her.

Me: That is one reason why you like coming here, to get away from her.

Gabrielle: Yes. I can't stay long, because soon I will be having my lunch; so may I come another day?

Coping with the concept of the retaliatory object relative to oral sadism and ambivalence

Anxiety relative to the enjoyment of me and my toys, free from Susan

Here she was showing the usual anxiety
about living a life that is separate from Susan,
and having me to herself which is so important
to her. She went on: "I am sorry we were a bit
early, because I could not stay at home any
more, because I was longing to go to Mr. Winnicott. Susan terribly wants to go to Mr. Winnicott. She says: 'No! No! No!'; instead of 'yes'
she says 'no' and she wakes up in the night. She
wakes every baby up. It's horrible. She doesn't
wake me. I would not even hear. I can hardly
hear her. She says? 'Mummy mummy dafferdil
daddy daddy dafferdil mummy mummy map-
pin bone chicken.' "

Gabrielle was placing houses, like the
words, in a row, with a tower at one end. I think
this was a train. She commented, "Dogs are not
allowed to eat little bones because they have
some kind of a splinter inside them." Here she
was rubbing her hand under the train wheels in
a way which seemed to be demonstrating something that she does to herself. She said: "Hurt
very much. Have you a dog?"

*Toward
masturbation*[2]

Me: No.
Gabrielle: Granny has, it's called Bunny.

She had the *toys arranged in a scatter so
that each one was separate.*[3] I pointed this out
to her, and she said: "Yes," and then something

[2] See letter from mother, immediately following Second Consultation.
[3] Cf. disparate toys on her side of the line, when establishing her own identity;
see Seventh Consultation.

about: "bang up again." She touched my knee, but jumped away, saying: "I must just go out to daddy. I'll come back. I want to bring my doll." This was a very big doll called Frances. She would bring it back for me to shake hands with. She was fondling my shoe. Anxiety had manifested itself along with the affectionate contacts. The separation of each object from every other was a defense in this respect. Contact with me was central, and various kinds of guilt appeared relative to this—guilt that there is no Susan, guilt also about destruction of the object that has been found—so that behind this separating of the objects from each other there could be said to be an internal chaotic state made of the bitten-up object parts.

Separation of objects each from the other, with its opposite: bumping up against

Gabrielle: One evening I had a bad dream. It was about. . . . I shut my eyes. I saw a beautiful horse. It was called Stallion. It had gold on its ears and on its mane. It is so very beautiful. Gold, nice shiny gold [she put her hand between her legs]. The beautiful horse was coming and trampling on the wheat [she explained that wheat is a sort of corn].

Me: You are describing a picture of daddy on mummy making new babies, something to do with love.

Gabrielle: Yes.

Me: Perhaps where mummy has hair [referring to the wheat].

Report of a dream

She then said something about going into daddy and mummy's room to stop the horse trampling on the wheat, by getting in between them. She added: "Sometimes I am allowed to stop for supper," giving me in this way a reality setting for the dream in which she prevents intercourse — also a setting in which Susan is excluded, Susan being a complication she cannot properly allow for.

Gabrielle: We like sitting up, but in the morning we get tired because of it [taking up a tiny figure]. This man can't sit down. Daddy [cf. Stallion] is beautiful.

Gabrielle now had the toys arranged in a different way, with all the trees and figures standing up and a general sense of life in the arrangement.

Gabrielle: Daddy is beautiful. There is a picture up on the wall at home of two people walking along and someone just standing there.

I compared this with the dream where something is trampling on something.

Me: You came to tell me about the stallion that tramples on the wheat.

The work of the session

Gabrielle rearranged the toys so that there was a long, curved row of houses and another long line of houses seeming to drive right into the curve. She said something about Susan, who would destroy everything, in this way using Susan for a projection of her own unwanted destructive ideas.

Gabrielle: Susan opens ladies' handbags and takes the powder out and smells it, and she disturbs mummy when she is dressing. It's terrible.

   Me: It makes you want to shoot her.

Gabrielle: Mummy has a beautiful statue.

Here she put the dog (lamb) standing up, but she also took the other large, soft dog (faun) and started squeezing the sawdust out of its belly, continuing the destructive activities of the last session. She put her finger in very deliberately, pulling out the stuffing, which went over the floor. Her anxiety showed by her making contact with father, going out to tell him not to call "ready."

   Me: You have come today without being called.

She seemed pleased, as if something had been corrected, and went back to the toy arrangements, standing the animals and everything else up on the carpet. There was something now about a secret, and her hands went between her legs.

Gabrielle: Dear Mr. Porter. I was reading Everybody's and got carried on to Crewe. I will have it on the train. I will carry Mr. Crewe.

She was rearranging the toys in an ordered way, repeating "Reading Everybody's got carried on to Crewe."[4]

Gabrielle: Don't wait for me. Go to Alabama with a banjo on my knee. Beautiful music.

I could recognize the various tunes. She was singing now in a happy, carefree way, introducing her own variations.

Gabrielle: Would you like to pass me some-things? He is doing his brrrrrrh [meaning feces]

and she emptied the sawdust, as much as she could, out of the faun's belly.

Gabrielle: Look at him!
    Me: He has done much brrrrrh on the basket and on to the carpet.
Gabrielle: I'm sorry. Do you mind?
    Me: No.
Gabrielle: It does smell.
    Me: You are taking out his secrets. He still has some more brrrrrrh.
Gabrielle [after a while]: Is it time to go? Piggle made an awful smell.
    Me: Making a smell is giving away secrets [she put some of the brrrrrrh in the tractor and in the wagons and every-

This marks the end of the flight from intestinal fantasy to the idea of adults and their capacity to give birth to real babies, i.e., acceptance of what is inside, between eating and defecation

---

[4] "Oh Mr. Porter, whatever shall I do? I was reading Everybody's and got carried on to Crewe" (an advertizing jingle of pre-World War I).

where].Golden stuff [joining it up with the picture].

Gabrielle took all the toys and gathered them together, making an agglutination.

>   *Me:* Now they are all in contact with each other and nothing is alone.

She said something about the emptied dog (fawn):

Contrast with disparateness

>   *Gabrielle:* Be kind to him. Let him have all his milk and food.
>   *Me:* You will have to go soon now.
>   *Gabrielle:* I will have to go now [and she pressed the sawdust into the wagon]. I will take a train back. Now we will have to go. I will just leave you with all the mess.

She also left her very large doll Frances, but came back and fetched it, finding me (deliberately) still sitting on the floor in the very considerable mess she had made. She did not actually take any train away with her.

COMMENTS

1. Easy re-establishment of relationship deliberately communicated in playing.

2. My birthday. Interpretation: death-day.

3. Separateness (disparate toys), and bumping and banging in contact.

4. Guilt because of destructive impulses toward the good object.

5. The same in terms of man and woman in sexual experience.

6. Identification with the man, sadism toward the belly and the breast (container).

7. Secret smells and mess; golden and beautiful.

8. Inside stuffs freed from doing double duty—i.e., from representing (delusionally) her inner psychic reality, now communicable in dream form.

LETTER FROM THE MOTHER

"Gabrielle would like to see you again; she has asked me over some time now if you could see her, and I have been rather dilatory about letting you know.

"In some ways she seems well in herself— she has started to go to a nursery school for two and a half hours every day, and she loves it. She plays *beside,* rather than *with,* children, and this satisfies her. However, she has many anxieties, and we feel that she often has difficulties in using the whole of herself, but that a part seems to remain riveted and frozen.

"I shall give you a description of the day that led her most urgently to ask to see you, just in case this throws any light.

"The night before, she asked to suck my breasts. She had asked several times and I had always shelved it, but this time let her do so. She sucked with great enjoyment, in all kinds of different ways and positions, with occasional anxieties that she was biting me.

"The night after that, she had a very bad dream, which made her leave her room, and she was found sobbing under a rug on a settee next morning. Asked me whether witches have breasts. She said that she was so naughty that she would grow up into a robber, and Susan would be the robber chief.

"On the evening she asked me whether I had a long wee. Said she thought I had. I said I was a woman like she was going to be. 'I suppose you wear skirts and blouses' (she said doubtfully). I asked where she thought I got my long wee from. 'The daddy.' 'And the daddy?' — 'From his students.' — 'Could I see Dr. Winnicott?' — Later: 'Is it *Doctor* Winnicott? Does he make people better?' — 'Doesn't he make you better?' — 'No, he just listens to me. He does not make me better.'

"When we were away recently she slept in a room next to ours, with a connecting door. This was very exciting to her, and caused a great deal of trouble."

LETTER FROM THE MOTHER

"Thank you for the appointment for Gabrielle. She has been setting off for London to see you several times lately, and could only be persuaded with difficulty that she cannot go to you just when she wants it.

"Seen from outside, she seems well in many ways, but she is often depressed. 'No, I am not tired, just sad.' When pressed she will say it's

because of the black mummy, but will say no
more.

"Of late there has been continuous talk
and speculation about 'babies.' "

ELEVENTH CONSULTATION
(June 16, 1965)

Gabrielle (now three years, nine months) was brought by her father. She came in, in a state which could be called shy delight. Immediately she went to the toys in the usual way; she talked all the time in a very adenoidal voice, starting off with: "The udder evening I woke and I had a dream about a train. I called Susan next door. Susan seems to understand. She has had her birthday and she is now two." She went on playing with the trains, saying: "Now we need a carriage because trains don't go without carriages. Susan understands better" (implying better than D.W.W.).

Compare initial shyness

Gabrielle: She can't talk.
    Me: Would it be better if I didn't talk?
Gabrielle: If you would listen, that would be best [she was in the process of joining up parts of the train].
    Me: Shall I talk or listen?
Gabrielle: Listen! Sometimes me and Susan are quiet as mice. This carriage won't fit

Cue

135

into this. . . . [One of the hooks
would not go into the eye.] I am
doing this very long. We saw some
trains that hadn't got these behind
them.

Gabrielle's hand caressed the engine she
had put at the back of the train she was build-
ing. She was making a lot of breathing noises,
perhaps due to the adenoids and the necessity to
breathe through her mouth.

She now wanted me to help her with this
difficult hook, and I did manage to enlarge the
eye with my pocket scissors. While I had my
back to her she said: "Dr. Winnicott you have
got a blue jacket on and blue hair." I looked
round and saw that she was looking at the world
through the blue Optrex eyeglass, the one that
had been highly significant the last time she
came to me (in fact there were now two of
these). She now resumed her train play, putting
aside bits of trains that could not be hitched on
because of defects. She was whispering "puffer
train"; "look what was in here"; "yes, it's
funny!" — and she had put the other blue Optrex
cup on one of the trucks. She then had four
train systems; she put these glasses to her eyes
again and sang: "Two little buckets sitting on a
wall./Two little buckets hanging on a wall."
She was very unself-conscious, ending the song
in a squeak: "Ten little pussies went. . . ."

She joined bits of train to make one main
train, whispering and talking to herself, putting

*Implying the
transfer of
her feelings
about the
Optrex cup
to the whole
of me.
Identification
with the
analyst*

words together, and sometimes using nursery rhymes.

Gabrielle: Sally go round the chimney pot on a Saturday afternoon. Look at this long train now.

Me: What are you telling me now about this train? [thinking of my role as listener].

Gabrielle: It is long [she said this several times] like a snake.

Me: Is it like a big daddy thing?

Gabrielle: No, a snake. Snakes are poisonous if they bite. If you don't suck the blood out, the man will die. It might bite me. Yes, if I move. If I don't move, he won't bite me. I must be careful then [pause]. This is a very long train [searching out more trucks]. Puffer puff — blow — blow — blow — puffer puffer puffer [sings] puffs blows.

Here is an adumbration of fellatio and oral sadism (see below) appearing in projected form

Gabrielle went through "Sally put the kettle on" — altering the last line to something to do with, "Susan take it off again."

Gabrielle: Susan can't say: "All gone," so she says: "Dad all don." She's silly.

Me: You were two once, and now you are four.

Gabrielle: No, three and three-quarters. I'm very big. I'm not quite four.

Me: Do you want to be four?

Gabrielle: Yea. Haha!

She took the broken circular object and played with it, singing.

Gabrielle: Pat-a-cake, pat-a-cake, Baker's man,
Bake me a cake as fast as you can.
Me: What's the hurry?
Gabrielle: Well it has to be ready before night-time when everyone is in bed. Pull it and pat it and make it with p. Put in the oven for Susan and me [this she repeated, substituting mummy for Susan].
Me: Perhaps the pancakes are mummy's breasts?
Gabrielle: Yes [said unconvincingly—perhaps I should have said "yams"]. Will it come off? [she was trying to fix something at the end of the train]. It won't come on.

Gabrielle then counted up from one, leaving out some, reaching up to "eleventeen." There was a climax at eight, and it all had to do with the length of the train: "What will it be if I put another one in, nine? No it will be four" (this seemed like nonsense). "Hey, I can't go right in here." She then reached beyond me to get the soft animal (faun) whose insides she had nearly emptied out last time. She took this animal now over beyond the toys and systematically emptied out a good deal more of the stuffing, making a considerable mess. She verbalized this to some

As if she kept track of the number of sessions so far

extent, talking about collecting stuff from the doggie's insides and making a mess on the floor.

Gabrielle: It's going to do some more. I'll open the eiderdown. He'll have to do some more. It smells lovely. A lovely perfume smell. Why do insides smell good? Well, you see here, it's from a a haystack [collecting sawdust in one of the eyebaths]. It's the next-door boy's birthday today.

The child talked about his having been called Bernard, another boy called Gregory, and so on. By now there was a great mess of sawdust (or dried hay, or whatever it was).

Gabrielle: Now there's a mess all over. Can you see me [eyeglass to eye]?

Something bumped on the floor.

Gabrielle: It went pomp on the floor and gave the room a shaking. To wake the trains up so that they go again. We went in a train. London's so far away.

Me: What you are telling me by the train is that its bits make up Piggle, three and three quarters; and it's also daddy's long thing.

It was a very long train now (she had joined up the carriages and trucks). Manipulating the train she made it go backwards a little and said: "Our train went backwards" (i.e., the trains she and her father came up on. She had made the train into a wide curve). "This carriage needs string."

We arranged it so that she could pull the train. She talked about tying it up, and made jokes on the word *snapper*, perhaps because I was using scissors to get her some string free of the tangled-up mass of string. Gabrielle said, "A big wee; snipped off; no" (obscure area here). This had to do with a dream of trains. I asked her for more about the dream.

Gabrielle: Pulling a long train; aw, it comes off, make it try and hit something, oh dear. Now start all over again.

She pushed together the whole train deliberately and, in this way, broke up the train into a muddle, away from her and toward me. In the dream it starts all over again.

Gabrielle: One day there was a witch, a sea witch, a woman witch, not a man witch [play on words]; baby-hugger-horrible. I can't find the little hole for this to go through. Women have two holes, one for wee and the other for babies [here she put a train on a horsecart, as if mocking]. Daddy wee-wee inside a girl hole; look it's come off! [referring to the funnel of the train].

Now Gabrielle told me of children putting stones on a railway. A man got a horrible bump. The children were naughty. They liked doing it. Were they angry with the daddy wee-wee?

Gabrielle: Yes. It was the men who were trying to work on the railway, not the engine driver.

She was manipulating the steering wheel of the tractor, saying: "I am going to sit on the tractor seat" (and she did, though the tractor seat is only about four inches long): "I'm driving it" (the tractor was under her, and in proximity with her "girl hole"). She made the tractor go right up to D.W.W. "I can't get up. I've got it up." Here she did some very quick play, first putting the tractor over the position of my penis, and then going quickly up to the breasts (I knew she had recently seen mother's breasts and had had a big reaction). She was playing with words all the time.

Gabrielle: Tipple, topple, pitter patter, raindrops, I hear thunder, I hear thunder. Pitter patter raindrops. Here's a man with glasses [I had glasses on, as did little toy man]. He's going to drive the tractor. This man looks funny.

I said she was laughing at me as a man with a wee-wee instead of breasts. She bent the man figure right back and pushed her finger on the place where the man's penis would be, with the man completely in her power, saying: "Draw on the electric bulb!"[1] I drew a man's face as before—she said something which included "a big wee, like a breast."

Gabrielle: What's this? What's this?
      Me: You are angry with the man's wee-wee; he ought not to have it.
Gabrielle: The man's a big robber; he's horrible.

I said she was talking about the man using his wee in a horrible way to make babies with (remembering the emptying out of the doggie).

Here she started very deliberately on a new play, arranging a long row of houses and another row at an angle so that there was a courtyard (it was time, but she was not yet ready to go).

      Me: What have I listened to today?
Gabrielle: One of the neighbors says, "You tell me and I'll tell you."

She repeated this several times because she was amused. She ignored my request that she should go, because she had not finished. She made a deliberate search for the little animals, and when she had found them she put them in the middle of the courtyard.

I made my main interpretation here, and it seemed to be what she wanted.

      Me: The man is a robber. He robs the mother of her breasts. He then uses

[1] See Tenth Consultation.

Control of a man: defense against anxiety re sadistic split-off male sex function

Penis envy

A good joke

Main work of the session

> the stolen breast as a long thing (like the train), a wee-wee, which he puts into the girl's baby hole, and in there he plants babies [animals in the play]. So he doesn't feel so bad about having been a robber.[2]

She was now quite ready to go, and went for daddy.

Gabrielle: We'd better go now because our train will be waiting for us to go, and we had better hurry.

And she was not to be put off when her father tried to explain that there was no hurry because they would have to wait anyway. Piggle looked very happy as she left with her father and did not need to wave goodbye more than quite ordinarily.

COMMENTS

1. D.W.W. to listen. Include control of D.W.W.

2. Control of split-off male sex function = fear of penis, including:

3. Penis-envy frankly displayed.

4. Interpretation of man and his male sex function including sex fantasy, i.e., end of split-off sex function.

5. Including man's reparation with respect

[2] See the work of Melanie Klein on reparation and male potency.

to guilt over aggression (see previous sessions
and her own depressive position).

LETTER FROM THE MOTHER   JULY 10, 1965

"Gabrielle has asked to see you again. She
has suddenly lapsed into misery and boredom,
after having been remarkably well.

"One of the things I have found a little
worrying is the savagery with which she hits
herself, when I have told her off, e.g., about
making a noise and waking up her sister. She is
exceedingly 'good' and then has sudden long-
ings for naughtiness at all costs. Her sister is
very difficult to stand up to, with a cry so full of
anger and crestfallen reproach, that Gabrielle
stands there with her hands over her ears when
she has stood her ground, and often gives in.
They get on exceedingly well, and share any
booty such as chocolate or biscuits quite spontaneously.

"Another matter I wanted to tell you
about; her thoughts about being a girl. She
asked me where the hole is where the baby goes
in, and then asked whether I also wanted to be a
boy; she very much wants to be a boy, but did
not elaborate why. At school, she says, she does
not like 'the boys.' I don't know how relevant
this is; we have mislaid our bathroom key, so
when their father has a bath, Gabrielle and
Susan crowd into the bath and get a bit excited."

LETTER FROM ME TO THE PARENTS

JULY 12, 1965

"I must ask you to tell Gabrielle that I cannot see her at the present moment. Things will have to wait till September.[3]

"I do not feel absolutely in despair about the way things are going. Children do have to work through their problems at home, and I would not be surprised if Gabrielle is able to find a way through the present phase. Naturally, she thinks of coming to me because she has done so on so many occasions, and I will certainly see her again, but not now."

LETTER FROM THE MOTHER   JULY 13, 1965

"I was only passing on Gabrielle's own request, not giving my own opinion as to her needs to see you. These I find almost impossible to assess, as I am much too involved.

"Gabrielle has been depressed and tearful, but I am certain that she is quite capable of working through this and other things from a short-term view. Whether in the long run enough of herself is available to her to make creative use of, is the really important thing, and one I also feel unable to assess. She sometimes appears to me a little spurious, not quite herself as if she had not invested all of herself in what she does and says. But perhaps this is not

---

[3] The summer of 1965 was an exceptionally demanding time and included a period of illness.

the moment to tell you about these long-term worries.

"The enclosed from Gabrielle is exactly according to her instructions."

NOTE FROM GABRIELLE (DICTATED)

"Dear Mr. Winnicott, Dear Mr. Winnicott, Dear Mr. Winnicott, I hope you are keeping well (I can't write)."

LETTER FROM THE MOTHER (TWO MONTHS LATER)

"Gabrielle appears quite well adjusted now, though I do not know on what basis. She has become a very organizing, controlling little girl, with many prudential considerations before she engages in any course of action.

"She loves her nursery school—she goes for two and one half hours every day—and she longs for a friend, but finds it difficult to make friends and usually plays alone, though she plays creatively. She seems rather thrown back on her little sister's company, and has become very intimate with her.

"She takes a much more benevolent view of her mother than formerly.

"As always, I am struck by her insight into people and situations (including into me) and by her ability to formulate this.

"When your name is mentioned, her face sets, and she changes the subject. This was her response also now when I told her that you rang up to inquire after her (I do not usually mention our telephone conversations though). A few moments after this she told me that she thought why the "Wattie"—our former much-loved domestic help—left, is because the Wattie ceased to like Gabrielle. She also says that the children at school do not like her.

"She went through a very rough time about the end of July, beginning of August; seemed very depressed and was up half the night. She could not at first believe that she could not see you. She had a recurrent dream that her mother and father were cut into little pieces, boiling in some container; whenever she shut her eyes the image returned, so she tried to keep awake.

"The following conversation I recorded on August 7th, after this had been going on for some time: 'The dream has come again, the cutting up one.' 'Can't you try and put them together, make them better?' 'No I can't. They are too small, in splinters; and it hurts me with the boiling water. So small like these little things that hurt in the mouth. I must go to Mr. Winnicott. *Dr.* Winnicott. Does he make ill people un-ill? I don't think he likes anybody as much as he likes me. He has a lot of delicate things there. I could not take Susan, she would break them.'

"Next day she said something about having managed to put the bits together, but someone always pulls them apart. I do not know the ultimate fate of this fantasy; it seems just to have subsided.

"A few days later she announced: 'I am afraid I wasn't such a nice girl as I am. I am a nice tidy girl; I tidy things.' She has been laying great stress on tidying things (which in some ways is a blessing in such an untidy family). I feel I am in the picture only on the most superficial level."

LETTER FROM THE MOTHER (THREE WEEKS LATER)

"Gabrielle has asked several times to see you. I have no idea with what degree of urgency.

"Previously she had asked me to tell you she was angry with you and not to ask you to see her. When I told her to tell you herself or dictate a letter, she said she was too shy.

"She has been very destructive lately; she urgently wants to find 'naughty' things to do, and proudly announces this. It usually takes the form of tearing up or cutting up things or messing them up. This is a new thing on the whole. She is much less anxious about things, I mean much less obviously so. She also spends quite a lot of time sucking her thumb and twisting her hair, so she must be in some trouble."

TWELFTH CONSULTATION
(October 8, 1965)

I was at the door when the father and child (now four years, one month) arrived by taxi. The father went straight to the waiting room, and I said: "Hullo Gabrielle." She fixed her eyes on me and then went straight into the room where the toys were stacked away under the shelf as usual. She had a rather heavy leather bag hanging over her shoulder on its leather strap. Having satisfactorily seen me, she sat on the floor and said: "Well let's look at the toys." She then took up the lamb.

Gabrielle: We've got one of these at home. I'm sorry we were so late, but the train stopped and stopped and stopped, and then the back of the train caught fire, but luckily no one was hurt [very grown-up language!]. And then train stopped for a long long time. Trains are supposed to go fast and not stop, but the train did stop.

149

While she was saying this she was putting a train together and then she was playing and talking to herself in a whisper.... She made a sort of huddle of short trains including a horse and wagon and a tractor. She was a bit puzzled that some of the carriages had no links, and I heard this reflected in her whisper ... "Can't join...." Somehow she fixed them or left them.

I was sitting this time on the chair, not on the floor (first time so), writing notes as usual. It was striking the way that she, as usual, had immediate confidence in me and the situation. She was like an illustration of "the capacity to be alone in the presence of someone," sitting on the floor, playing, muttering, and obviously conscious of me.

I noticed that by chance she touched my leg with her body as she bent over to get the new toys. This was not at all exaggerated, and there was no withdrawal from it when it happened. She is like this with her father. Sometimes she was sitting almost on my shoe talking to herself rather loud and making some train noises. After a quarter of an hour, she said: "Phew!" This meant that it was rather hot. By accident, she put her head against my knee quite naturally without exaggerating. I continued to say nothing. Her bag was still slung over her shoulder. Often one hand was on her bag while she propped herself up.

She arranged four long houses in a square and put another house in the center. I knew that this meant something important and had to do with her being able to be a container, and I associated it in my mind with her now carrying a bag. About here she took her bag off and then took her cardigan off, all the time being liable to rub against my knee as I sat in the chair. She said it was hot, which it was. Then she was playing with the singing-top remnant. Here was the first sign of faint anxiety, although in fact anxiety was not manifest during the whole hour. It showed by her looking round at me writing. This remnant of a singing top is one of several in the muddle of toys that has played an important part in the past. She took things out of another basket, each little bit separately, talking to herself, using her lips but not audibly except for certain words like "toys." Then she turned round and smiled, and I knew something special was happening. She had in fact found the old small-sized electric bulb that had played a big part in past sessions.

Gabrielle: Put a skirt round it.

I wrapped some paper round the bulb, and it was now a lady, and she put it on the book case in front of us.

> *Me:* Is that mummy?
> *Gabrielle:* No.

It is characteristic of this child that "yes" and "no" have exact meaning in the sessions.

> *Me:* Is that what Gabrielle wants to grow up into one day?

Gabrielle: Yes.

There was a little more contact with me, and I could detect anxiety from what was going on. I saw that she was rubbing a little car with her finger. I knew she was referring to masturbation, and I continued to say nothing.

Gabrielle: This car's a silly car. It goes this way
and that way and it isn't supposed to.

And she rolled it over and over in her hands. Then she took a tiny figure which she used as a female.

Gabrielle: This lady is always lying down. She
lies down again and again and again.
Me: Is that mummy?
Gabrielle: Yes.

I tried to get further information without success. She went on playing and then she said: "Now what have we got here?" She was talking to herself: "Please could I have this . . . and this . . . and this?" And then she said to some animals: "You stand up." She brought in the word black about one of the animals. "Black is nothing. What is it?"

I have been very interested in Gabrielle's use of the idea of black, and here was a new version of this theme.

Me: Is black what you don't see?
Gabrielle: I can't see you because you are black.
Me: Do you mean that when I am away
then I am black and you can't see

me? And then you ask to come and
see me and you have a good look at
me and I am light or something else
that isn't black?

Gabrielle: When I go away and look at you you
go all black don't you Dr. Winnicott?

Me: So after a time you have to see me so
as to bring me white again.

*Here black
is partly
a defense
i.e., it is not
not seeing me
when I am
absent
instead of
remembering
me in my
absence*

She seemed to have dealt with this idea,
and she went on with detailed playing. She was
trying to get a little figure to stand on a truck,
an impossible task, and in so doing she bumped
her head against my knee. I was not able to fully
understand what was happening.

Me: If there is a long interval, then you
begin to get worries about this black
thing which was me gone black, and
then you don't know what the black
thing is.

Here I was referring to the black mummy and
the black objects of her anxiety states.

Gabrielle: Yes [in a fairly convincing way].

Me: So when you came you had a good
look at me to bring me white again.

Gabrielle: Yes.

She now passed over to the matter of her
handbag, which was on the floor where she was
sitting.

Gabrielle: I have got a key in my handbag. It's
in here. I hope it's in there [and she

was feeling for it]. It unlocks your
door. I lock it for you if you want to
go out. You haven't got a key here,
have you?

She took a long time doing up the clasp of her
bag, muttering: "I can't; yes I can." She kept on
doing it up and overdoing the movement necessary. Then she accomplished this kind of
locking of her case and gave a sigh indicating
she had done a lot of work (working against
conflict).

She went back to the toys, contemplating a
small basket. I continued saying nothing except
what I have reported. She took the dog (lamb)
and pushed it in the belly. This reminded me of
what she had done the previous two or three
times, culminating in her making a big mess in
the previous session. She had poked her finger
in the belly of the other animal and had
emptied the contents all over the floor. She, of
course, was reminded of the same thing and she
said: "Mr. Winnicott, where's that dog?" I
pointed to a big envelope which in fact contained the empty dog, and she said: "Oh!"

She was handling the car again and
putting it to her nose and mouth. She took a
pencil which happened to be a red crayon,
banged it into her own belly, and then used it to
color the skirt of the lamp lady and she gave the
lamp a hat (the Optrex cup). She was banging
the head of the bulb with the pencil, perhaps
trying to color it, and then she took the skirt off

*Preview of
puberty*

the bulb, which she had said represented herself as a grown-up lady, and started scratching underneath it with the pencil. Afterward she readjusted the skirt. There was now red color on the skirt. She then put a little figure against a big house.

> *Me:* What is that?
> *Gabrielle:* He's shooting into the church [then she said what had been in her mind all the time]. What happens to the dog in the bag? Where is he in there?
> *Me:* Have a look if you want to.
> *Gabrielle:* All right.

She investigated with utmost caution, taking a lot of time, and even in the end did not get it out of the envelope. Eventually she screwed it up and put it back in its place under the shelf saying: "His nose has come off; he has lost his nose; a dog in a bag."

> *Me:* Last time you got all the inside out of it and let it go all over the floor.
> *Gabrielle:* Yes.

I started to play about with interpretations: "It is a breast if I am mummy, or a wee-wee if I am daddy." She very definitely said: "No, it's a wee-wee-thing" (the "no" meaning not a breast).

> *Me:* You wanted to make a baby out of the mess.
> *Gabrielle:* Yes.

Me: But you don't quite know how to.
Gabrielle: No.

She was now playing with a train, and began to show some anxiety, although not in a manifest way.

Gabrielle: We go in the train soon now. We left
            Susan at home. Susan may be very
            cross because we have been away so
            long.
Me: You began to be a bit frightened
       then to think of you having daddy all
       to yourself in the train, especially
       when you think of what you want to
       do to him, because you want to do to
       daddy the same as you were showing
       me when you took the stuff out of the
       dog. When you love me it makes you
       want to eat my wee-wee [this has first
       turned up in the fear of the biting
       snake, see above].

She said to one of the carriages she was manipulating: "Don't hold on to my skirt!" And then she began to put on her cardigan, an operation that took considerable time.

Me: You really were a bit frightened just
       then when you thought of eating the
       inside out of the wee-wee.
Gabrielle: Yes. Katchou! [by which she really
            meant, "Isn't it hot, and how tired
            I am"].
Me: Do you want help?

Gabrielle: No.

I then made quite a lot of interpretations.

> *Me:* You got a bit frightened thinking of the black Winnicott, who was there but couldn't be seen, or really he just wasn't there and you were angry with him for not being there.
>
> You were frightened too about the idea of the nose that was off the dog because that was biting off my wee-wee. You were angry with me for not being always yours.
>
> You are frightened to think that when you love me you tear the stuffing out of my wee-wee!

Gabrielle: Yes.

> *Me:* If it's the mother's breast, you get the stuff out to get fat and to grow, but when it's a wee-wee you really want to have stuff to make into babies.

Gabrielle: Ow! Yes.

> *Me:* The key in your bag is like having a place in you for storing up what you get out of me, a wee-wee that is yours for keeps, something that might become a baby.

All this time the cardigan operation was in progress. We had had three quarters of an hour, and she said something about everything being finished now. The cardigan was on. She was tired. She got up, using her hand on her bag. She opened the bag and took the key and scrabbled on the lock with it.

> *Me:* If you were a man, you would push your wee-wee into the hole which the skirt covers.
>
> *Gabrielle:* Do you know I'm going to have some apple juice in the train? Daddy said we must remember to bring back some for Susan.
>
> *Me:* You feel a bit frightened to really have me all to yourself. When you have me or daddy alone you have the wee-wee going in and making babies, and so you don't have to go at it and get out the stuff that's inside it, so you don't feel so awful about that, but then you feel Susan will be jealous because it's so good.

Anxiety. Defensive regression into ideas

Gabrielle resumed her play with toys. All this time there had been no manifest anxiety, only anxiety the observer could postulate on the basis of behavior and verbal remarks. She played with two, then three, then four objects.

I interpreted that she was showing me she could put two people together, and she could get in between daddy and mummy to join or separate them, and that would be three. But it was more than she could do to fit in Susan too — a fourth didn't fit in. This seemed all right.

> *Gabrielle:* Mr. Winnicott, I'm just going to the toilet. I'll be back in a minute.

And she went out leaving her bag on the floor with the toys, in complete confidence. She carefully shut the door (which, when she came earlier on, used to be difficult to shut; it had been mended, and she seemed to notice the change). She came back in three minutes, carefully shut the door again, and resumed her playing.

Gabrielle [diving into the bag]: Put it; where did I put it? Where did . . . ? [repetitively]? The key is supposed to be in there, but it isn't. Oh, there it is [it was lying among the toys].

So she took the key and tried it on my door (the latch covers the keyhole, and it can't be moved because the paint is stuck. I tried to help, but failed).

Me: You could try the other side [outside].

Gabrielle: But I'd lock myself out [joke intended]. And I wanted to be inside. Then when I tried to go I'd unlock it outside... [implying: this idea just wouldn't work]. I wouldn't be able to get in to let myself out. I could only get out if I lock myself in. And soon....

Me: It'll be time to go soon.

Gabrielle: Yea. If I lock the outside, I lock you in.

Me: And have me like the key in the bag.

[This scarcely needed saying.] It's time now.

She was quite ready to go, so she collected her handbag, with the key safely inside it, in the correct compartment. But she dropped a postcard from the bag. I told her about this, and she showed it to me: "Some bunnies walking across a river; we do that sometimes when we go for a walk." She went out and shut the door using her magic key, saying "bye-bye," and this went on through the closed door after she had collected her father, and when the two went off together.

COMMENTS

Me on chair—first time.

1. Container theme with internalized object = D.W.W. held and preserved.

2. Herself as girl in skirt.

3. Female onanistic clitoral activity.

4. Idea of woman always lying down (preparatory to menstrual theme).

5. Black as denial of absence (looking as denial of not seeing), covering up the memory of the absent object.

6. The lock of her bag. Key in door. Red on skirt (menses). Idea of female genital erotism—vulval, vaginal.

7. Caution re sadistic attack on the faun's (or dog's) belly.

8. Baby out of men. Immaturity to be tolerated.

9. Theme of fourth person—no place for her sister (Susan).

LETTER FROM THE MOTHER

"I have wanted to thank you very much for sending me the typescript of your last session with Gabrielle. It is most generous of you, and I am pleased that you knew how very much I would enjoy reading it.

"I think my husband told you on the phone that she has been much more serene since her last interview with you—less thumb sucking, very few bouts of destructiveness, and a humorous contemplation of her foibles.

"It cropped up in my mind the other day how we always write to you what is wrong with Gabrielle, not what has gone right and fallen into place; but at the time it is this that seems urgent.

"I would like to tell you—though you may know this—how much writing to you has helped me; somehow to give form to my perplexities and fears, with the knowledge that they would be received with great understanding; and the feeling of being in relation with you. I am sure all this helped me to work through our anxieties about Gabrielle and again to find our right relationship with her. My anxieties were very intense at the time of Susan's birth—I forget whether I told you that I have a brother, whom I greatly resented, who was born when I was almost exactly the same age as Gabrielle was when Susan was born."

LETTER FROM THE MOTHER

"Your letter came as I was sitting down to write to you. Gabrielle seems to have been well; little of that desolate thumb sucking, and she plays wholeheartedly and finds her own games.

"Two or three days ago she complained of bad dreams: 'Dr. Winnicott doesn't help.' — And then: 'How did the men put up the television aerial again when it had blown down?'

"Next day at lunch: 'The more I go to Dr. Winnicott, the more bad dreams I have.' I, a bit pompously: 'Perhaps they want to tell you something and you should listen to them.' 'I don't want to.' To Susan: 'We'll send Dr. Winnicott a knife to cut his dreams up.' To me: 'Why *Doctor* Winnicott?' (This she has asked frequently.) — 'Because he *is* a doctor.' Then play around with the word 'docdoc' which is Susan's word for chocolate.

"After lunch she dictated the enclosed letter. Later she said: 'Dr. Winnicott will think it funny to get this letter' — I: 'Is it meant to be funny, or very serious?' — 'A bit of both.' "

LETTER FROM GABRIELLE (DICTATED)

"We'll send you a knife to cut your dreams up, and we'll send our fingers to lift things up, and we'll send you some balls of snow to lick when the snow comes, and we'll send you some crayons to draw a man with. We'll send you a suit to wear when you go to college.

"With best wishes to your flowers and your
trees and your fish in your fishpool.
                    Love from
                        (Signed) Gabrielle."
"We are coming to see you with best wishes in
our heads."

(Actually I have no garden, but a small roof
garden can be seen through the back window of
the consulting room.)

LETTER FROM THE MOTHER

"Since I last wrote to you—only three or
four days ago—Gabrielle has been very sad,
lying on the floor sucking her thumb a lot, has
been tearful at the least provocation, and
unable to sleep at night. She has asked urgently
to see you. She has asked me several times what
she sent you in the letter she wrote to you, said
she had forgotten.

"The day after she wrote it, she was lying
on the floor with her thumb in her mouth.
'Tired?'—'No, sad.'—'?'—'About Dr. Winnicott, about Dr. W.'s wee.'—'I want to see
Dr. W. tomorrow. This time I will really tell
him what's the matter.'—'Lucky that you know,
most people don't.'—'I don't know, but I can
always tell him.'

"She has 'accidentally' dropped a basket of
apples on Susan from the top of the stairs and
broken her telephone. Afterwards she is very
fierce with herself, gets Susan to smack her, and

hits herself with great intensity. I find the fierceness of her self-recriminations a bit frightening, though they have not been in evidence again except very lately.

"P.S. On rereading this I feel I have given much too dark a picture. What I have described is just what emerged very recently rather suddenly, though along with all this I feel she is generally in a good way since her last session with you."

THIRTEENTH CONSULTATION
(November 23, 1965)

There was a rather special entry, charac-
terized by shyness; Gabrielle was now four
years, three months. When she came into the
room she shut the door and went straight to the
toys. I was sitting again on a chair, writing on
the table.

Gabrielle: Come out [and she brought all the
toys out on the floor, talking to
herself a good deal]. The church goes
there, doesn't it, Mr. Winnicott?
[There were special arrangements of
houses.] The little houses in a row
and the big houses in another row.

We talked about these together as rows of children and grown-ups.

Gabrielle: Yes, these are the grown-ups, and
these here are the children [and so
on].

Then she apportioned the children to the
grown-ups.

Gabrielle: Do you know when Susan was waiting for supper she fell out of the
pram and cut her lip. She was eating
her supper. Her lip was bitten. It was
cured. Isn't that funny? Cured.

Me: Do you get cured?

Gabrielle: No. I had a cut which I scratched
for a long long time.

She was indicating that she was the opposite of Susan, keeping her sores open. I could see
that she was talking about me in my various
roles.

Me: Susan hasn't been to see me.

(I knew that she had often felt like bringing
Susan, but that it was very important to her that
she not bring Susan and have me all to herself.)
She went on playing, and said: "Now look, it
came off the train; I can mend it myself." And
she did.

Me: You can be a mender, so you don't
need me as a mender now. So I am
Mr. Winnicott.

Gabrielle: Some men were doing a mending job
on the train. Do you know there was
no seat and we had to stand and we
walked and walked along and then
we found a place and we sat somewhere where there was a bag; someone had left their bag there.

She was arranging two trucks, sometimes

head to head and sometimes tail to tail. Then she said: "All the King's Horses could not put...."

> *Me:* They could not mend Humpty Dumpty.
> *Gabrielle:* No, because he was an egg.
> *Me:* You feel you can't be mended.[1]
> *Gabrielle:* Every night Susan wants an egg, she is so fond of them; I am not very fond of eggs. Susan is so fond of eggs she eats nothing but eggs. Isn't that funny?

Here she was in trouble about actual mending.

> *Gabrielle:* I have nowhere to fasten this. There is no hook. Can we find one?

There was a special arrangement of toys with various trains, trucks, and houses in parallel lines, orderly but not obsessionally accurate. Gabrielle commented, "Dr. Winnicott has got a lot of toys for me to play with," and she continued manipulating the trains, sorting them out of the muddle they were in.

> *Gabrielle:* The hook's out of this one; isn't that a silly-billy? I am mending it [and she did, very skillfully]. I really can put it in again.
> *Me:* Gabrielle is a mender too.
> *Gabrielle:* Daddy can mend things; we are both clever. Mother's not clever at all. At

---

[1] I think this was wrong; I should have waited for developments.

school I made a tractor for myself
and so I made one for Susan too.
While making it I was getting full of
glue. There was a mess of glue. It
was a nice tractor. One for Susan,
but I left it at school. Then it was
half-term and I could not get it. Do
you know Mr. Winnicott the train
went slowly, but it didn't stop all the
way to London [snow on the ground
today]. Then it went fast again.

Suddenly Gabrielle noticed the big bowl on
the shelf above her head.

Gabrielle: I like that bowl with a Chinese picture on it.

And she worked out all the details of the children playing games. We had to turn it round
and round. She said: "One of the children has
fallen down." She noticed everything and was
pleased with it.

Gabrielle [singing]: I haven't seen you for a
long time so I was shy when I came to
see you, and I shan't see you tomorrow nor tomorrow nor tomorrow.
Me: Are you sad about this?
Gabrielle: Yes. I like to see you every day, but
can't because I have to go to school.
I am supposed to go to school.
Me: You used to come here to be
mended, but now you come because
you like it. When you came to be

mended you came whether you had to go to school or not. But now you just like it, you can't come so often. That is sad.

Gabrielle: When I come to see you I am your visitor. You are my visitor when you come to Oxford. Isn't that strange? Perhaps you will come after Christmas.

Me: Is there anything to be mended about you today?

Gabrielle: No, I don't break any more. Now I break things up into pieces. This screw went in.

Me: Yes, you mended it yourself, and you can mend yourself.[2]

Gabrielle: Today Susan got into the dog box. This is a new toy.

She was stepping on the elephant, and the elephant squeaked.

Here she asked me to help her mend the train that she was in difficulties with.

Gabrielle: You are a doctor, a real doctor, that is why you are called Dr. Winnicott.

Me: Do you like to be mended or do you like to come for pleasure?

Gabrielle: For pleasure, because then I can play more [she said this very definitely]. I can hear someone whistling outside.

---

[2] I could have said, "You have a Winnicott mender inside you that you carry around with you," etc.

I did not hear this and I said: "Or was it me writing?"

Gabrielle: No. Someone's hooting now [true]. There are not enough hooks. When we were coming to you we were a bit early, so we walked around, so I must buy something for Susan and mummy. I like Susan and mummy.

Me: Here there is just Gabrielle and me. Is Susan cross when you come and see me?

Gabrielle: Do you know Susan ... she likes to watch me dance. How old is she? She is two. I am four. Next birthday I will be five and Susan will be three.

By this time she had nearly all the toys arranged in parallel lines, about ten or a dozen of these lines, and one set of three houses set at an angle.

Gabrielle: Dr. Winnicott, I just go to the toilet. You look after the toys. Don't let Daddy in.

She carefully shut the door as she went out, and was away three minutes.

Gabrielle: There. Mr. Winnicott I am going to stay a little bit longer than I usually do. I can play more if I have more time. I don't need to rush away.

Capacity for self-indulgence, but it also stirs anxiety

Me: Sometimes you feel frightened about something, and then you feel you want to go suddenly.

Gabrielle: Because it gets late. I can't undo this [I undid it for her]. Did you think this could go up there? [i.e., on the shelf by the portrait of the seven-year-old girl]. This could go up there too. Don't take them down will you — leave them there.

Me: Till you come next time. You feel that this gives you some hope of coming to me again.

Gabrielle: For all the time.

Then she looked at the portrait, mounted as it is in an oval mount, and said: "Look, she's in an egg."

Me: If she hadn't got a place to be she would be like Humpty Dumpty and go to pieces; but you have a place here where you can be.

She then gave me a lecture on eggs.

Gabrielle: If one breaks an egg without boiling it, when it is soft, it runs all over and everything gets dirty, but if one boils it hard and opens it, it just crumbles.

Me: I put an egg round Gabrielle and she feels all right.

Gabrielle: Yes.

She then took all the blue houses and put them in a circle with the red one in the middle, saying: "I am going to make a row of houses like this," and she put all the houses up against each other in a close row.

Gabrielle: If I see any more, I will put them in
        the row.

She was now collecting little people and
trees and animals: "A lot of things" (talking all
the time). She stood them up on the carpet as
far as possible. I could not hear what she was
saying well because she was talking to herself,
happy, easy, contented, creative, and imagi-
native. She had her back to me, and said something like: "I leave it like that. Mr. Winnicott
can I take this one and this one and this one? I
will bring them back. I will take two. I will leave
three or four for you. I have got three." (In fact,
at the end she had no need to take anything,
and had apparently forgotten the matter.)

Gabrielle: Whose turn is it to clean the bath?

There seemed to be a complex answer to this. It
had to do with rivalry with her sister over this
privilege. I did not take it for granted that there
is actually competition in this field at home,
looking at it from the parents' point of view. She
was making animal noises with some of the
animals in her hand.

Gabrielle: I like to clean the bath. You stay
        there [she was talking to the ani-
        mals]; not you, cow, you dog; you,
        cow, don't move at all; otherwise . . .
        you will be turned into witches.
    Me: Are you telling me a dream?
Gabrielle: Yes. I don't like it. It's horrible. To
        be turned into a little person with

teeny weeny feet. I turned into a giant in the morning. In the old days they didn't have shops.

Me: Well? [I encouraged her to go on].

Gabrielle: Well they didn't build shops, and if they sold lavender they went around and sang: "Who'll buy my lavender?" ... [singing]. A penny can spend. If Susan doesn't let somebody go up the stairs they have to pay six pence; isn't that a lot? ... I only make them pay one penny, not much is it?

I tried to get at what she was implying; it had to do with Susan being mean. Then she looked out of the window.

Gabrielle: Someone has a roof garden; that's funny; I can't get up there. I wonder how they water the flowers. They open the window with an iron stick and then put water up a chimney. They let it squirt all the flowers, and so everything gets watered. They put a spoon up the chimney and get all the water down, and then they do it again. [Then after a bit:] Is that your shed? Oh! You can't get to it, can you? Are those plastic flowers?

Me: No, they are real.

Gabrielle: I like plastic. Those are plastic [not really].

Me: Do you like real or plastic children and animals? [Here she opted for real].

Gabrielle: What is that wooden thing? [She had
                    spotted the end of a wooden cylindri-
                    cal ruler which another child had left
                    and which was among the books.]
                    Shall I bring it out?
      Me: Rightho.
Gabrielle: What is it for?
      Me: It's a ruler.

Gabrielle used the ruler as a rolling pin, as if it
was exactly what she had been looking for. First
of all it was to roll pastry. Here then was another role, that of cook, and I pointed this out
to her. The rolling developed into a game which
involved the whole room.

Gabrielle: When the woman comes to mend
                    things, the cook pretends to go to
                    sleep. You have to tell her to wake
                    up, and then she cooks some more.

She was trying to express what happened to the
other Winnicott roles when Winnicott is in one
role. The Dr. Winnicott who mends has gone
away for a holiday, so there is Mr. Winnicott
who cooks. When she needs mending, then
Dr. Winnicott comes back. She then went to
the gas fire.

Gabrielle: How do you light the gas fire?

I went over and showed her.

      Me: Now the mending Winnicott and the
                    cooking Winnicott have gone away,

and there is another Winnicott, the teaching Winnicott. And then there is the play Winnicott.

(For myself, in the setting, I was left with no doubt that the most valuable of the four roles is the play role, especially the one in which she is what I have called "alone in my presence.") There was another role that she reminded herself of, which had to do with the use of the wastepaper basket which could be said to be a Winnicott that helps her to get rid of what she has finished with (Dustbin Winnicott).

In the course of this, Gabrielle developed an organized game in which we rolled the ruler to and fro, and she came nearer and nearer, so that when she rolled the ruler it would bang against my knees. Here she was giving me a fifth way in which I had been important to her, someone that she bumped up against when she moved and who, in this way, could be used in her effort to distinguish what was not herself from what was truly herself. At one point when the ruler hit my knee, I turned over backwards and played the game with gusto to give her the satisfaction she needed. (It is not possible for a child of this age to get the meaning out of a game unless first of all the game is *played and enjoyed*. As a matter of principle, the analyst always allows the enjoyment to become established before the content of the play is used for interpretation.) It seemed as if Gabrielle had finished making her list of the ways in which she had used me. There was a period at the end in which she got the feeling that she was staying a little longer than usual *simply because she liked being with me when she was not feeling frightened,* and when she was able to get pleasure and to express in a positive way her relationship to me as a person. At the very end she added one more to her list of roles and said: "I will leave you to pack up." And so she left, being very careful to shut the door completely. She collected her father from the waiting room. On this occasion, I did open the door and say goodbye to them both, because in a way this was a gesture due to the father, and I felt that Gabrielle had finished what she wanted to tell me.

COMMENTS

1. Apportioning grown-ups to children — keeping me all to herself.

2. Development of the capacity to be her own "mender."

3. The train (analysis) had moved slowly, but went all the way to London = its destination.

4. Sadness over prospect of termination.

5. Secure about her place in my life.

6. Expression of having been solidly put together; she is now contented and creative.

7. Review of the various roles she used D.W.W. for.

LETTER FROM THE PARENTS
(WRITTEN ON HOLIDAY ABROAD)

"Gabrielle showed us your letter; how good of you to offer her an appointment.

"In many ways she has been in excellent form, robust, ebullient, and somehow creative in making up games and songs.

"Here she walks for hours, paddles in glacier water, enjoys going difficult ways, is well in touch with what she calls the 'bull girl' side of herself.

"In contact with strangers, especially men, she is shy, very affected, and responds with a distressing kind of spurious femininity. Strangers usually take much more readily to her sister Susan, who is curly-haired, extroverted and cheeky, than to the long inquiring looks of Gabrielle.

"Gabrielle is very close to Susan, handles her with great circumspection, cajoles her, is often the mediator between her and us. We are struck by how often she will try and get her way by deflecting Susan's attention or by some inventiveness, rather than by direct attack, though sometimes she is miserably, and helplessly, consumed by jealousy, and Susan can do nothing right. The other day, in the middle of a fierce fight, she suddenly kissed Susan and said: "But I like you." This is very different from Susan, who alternately looks up to Gabrielle fervently, and ruthlessly wants to destroy her superiority."

FOURTEENTH CONSULTATION
(March 18, 1966)

Gabrielle (now four years, six months) was brought by her father. She was obviously very pleased to be at the front door again. I stood still, and she gradually crept behind her father and came into the house hidden in this way. She went straight into the room and said: "I'll take my coat off," and she dropped it on the floor, immediately reaching for the toys. All the time she was talking while arranging them: "Dat; dat; der; oh, this has got tangled up." I realized she had a very stuffy nose. Soon she was also coughing, but otherwise she was very well physically.

Gabrielle: There. There. That's right!

She was fully engaged on the floor with her back to me, and she was linking up herself with other visits. Her words described what she was doing. At some point she said: "Is this really the way to do it or not?" She was displaying a superego with which she was easily identified. I said: "Yes I think so, but you can do it as you like."

179

Gabrielle went on about how she found the toys. As if she had left them in one packet, here she found two in one and two in another packet. She was trying to relate the carriages of the different kinds of train. Then she gave me something to fix as she had often done before. While I was doing this, she went over to a new toy on the bookcase, a little boy pulling a sleigh with a little girl on it.

Gabrielle: Is this from Christmas? It is pretty. Does it work?

Me: It only works if you imagine it working.

She then came back for what I had fixed.

Gabrielle: Thank you. I am going to get all the toys out.

She pulled everything into one big heap on the floor, renewing contact with her old friends.

Gabrielle: Look, this basket has got strawberry stains, and this one too.

So they were both strawberry baskets. With an exclamatory noise, she took the basket and emptied it out all over the other toys.

Gabrielle: This should be there, shouldn't it?

She picked out the donkey and cart which belonged on the bookcase.

Me: However did it get amongst all the other things?

Gabrielle: Once we took it from up there.

At this time she was in contact with my leg. She took the lamb and said: "What happened to the dog?" I handed her the envelope with the remains of the dog in it.

Gabrielle: Why is he in there? [She looked in.] You haven't had him mended yet. Aren't you naughty! You must really have him mended.

She then took the mysterious thing and said: "What's this?" We have never known what it is; probably part of a singing top.

Gabrielle: What's this? It's no good.

I said it was an oil tanker. She meant that it had no hooks. She was now coming to the end of renewing contact and she said: "Have you got a seashell anywhere? I want the sound." At this point she was sitting on my foot, and I talked about sitting on the beath with her father. It is as if she felt a link with whatever the beach meant to her and could not believe there was no sound of the sea.

She took a train with lots of wheels and enumerated the wheels, giving them colors. She fondled this engine lovingly and mouthed it and rubbed it across her thighs, and then over her head from back to front. This turned into a game, so that the engine came down over her face and fell onto the floor accompanied by a noise which had a climax. She tried to join this to a carriage, but did not succeed. She took the old man and the boy figures and sat them down saying: "You sit here. You sit there." Then, still renewing old details she said: "Could you draw [on the lamp]? Do a zigzag up and down. This is really a bulb." I dropped it.

Gabrielle: It should go in the light.

She had now practically finished with the toys and said to me: "Do you go to church?" I didn't know what to answer.

>   *Me:* Well, sometimes. Do you?
> *Gabrielle:* I would like to go, but mummy and
>   daddy would not like to. I don't
>   know why.
>   *Me:* Why do people go to church?
> *Gabrielle:* I don't know.
>   *Me:* Is it something to do with God?
> *Gabrielle:* No.

At this point she had a house she was mouthing. Now she brought something from the last time and said: "Where's that rolling thing?" This is the cylindrical ruler left by some other patient. I found it, and she now instituted a game which was the main part of her communication. It had roots in the past, and so we were able to use all sorts of short cuts. We kneel close together opposite each other in the front room. She rolls it to me and that kills me. I die and she hides. Then I come alive and I can't find her.

Gradually I made this into a kind of interpretation. By the time we had done it many times, and sometimes I was the one killing her, it became very clear that it had to do with sadness. For instance, if she killed me, then when I recovered I couldn't remember her. This was represented by her hiding, but I did eventually find her and then I said: "Oh I remember what it was I had forgotten." Although this game contained great pleasure, anxiety and sorrow were latent. Whoever was hiding had to leave a leg or something showing so that the agony of not being able to remember the lost person would not be prolonged or absolute. This was linked, among other things, with what happened when she did not see me over a long period of time. Gradually the game altered by specializing in its hiding aspect. For instance, I had to creep around the back of the desk where she was hiding, and then there were both of us there. Eventually it was fairly clear she was playing a game belonging to the idea of being born. At some point or other I made it clear that one reason why she was happy was that she had me alone. With regard to this detail, when she went out of the front door, the thing I heard her say to her father was: "Where's Susan?"

Working on the various reactions to separation and termination

Eventually I had to repeat a bursting out from under the curtains which seemed to be a kind of birth. Then I had to become a house, and she crept inside the house, rapidly becoming bigger until I could not contain her any longer and pushed her out. As the game developed, I said: "I hate you," as I pushed her out.

This game she found exciting. She suddenly got a pain between her legs and soon afterwards went out to pass water. The climax of this was getting in touch with the mother's need to be rid of the baby when it is too big. Associated with this is sadness about getting bigger and older, and finding it more difficult to play this game of being inside mother and getting born.

The session ended with a period in which she took the two curtains in the middle of the room and rushed backwards and forwards with them.

Gabrielle: I am the wind; look out!

There was not much hostility in the game, and I referred to breathing, the essential element in being alive and something which could not be enjoyed before birth.

At this point she was willing to go.

COMMENTS

1. In harmony with superego.
2. Evidence of potential capacity for genital enjoyment.
3. Working through the reactions to extended separations and preparing for termination.
4. The theme of birth.

FIFTEENTH CONSULTATION
(August 3, 1966)

Gabrielle (now nearly five years) arrived with her father, looking very well and very much a person. She was eager and full of a sense of anticipation. We talked a little about the holiday she had just had and about my house which was obviously in the hands of the plumbers. She went straight to the toys (while father went to the waiting room), and before I had taken my place in the low chair by the little table on which I have papers for taking notes, she said: "Nice doggie," catching hold of the part of the old singing top. "I'm four now—in August" (meaning that she was just coming up for five). There was a lot that happened that could not be noted down, as it was a kind of shorthand of coming to all the details in the muddle of toys.

Gabrielle: Ships. My knickers show. Where's the roller?

185

I showed her the cylindrical ruler she had used for the special game in the last session.

Gabrielle: That's nice. We'll play the game. . . .

I went over to the main part of the room, and we took up positions. I pretended I wasn't sure of the game, and she showed me how we roll it to and fro. As it hit my knees, I was killed and fell over dead and then there is a period of hide and seek. As I noted this she said: "You always write." And I told her how I made notes so that I could remember what happened in detail.

> *Me:* I remember it all without notes, but I can't get at the details, and I like to remember everything so that I can think it all over.

We had a to-and-fro game with the roller, followed by hide and seek, starting off by her killing me. Then I killed her and hid, for her to find. I said she was letting me know that she forgets me and that I forget her when we are apart or on holiday, but really we know we can find each other.

Separation without despair

She soon finished what she had to say in this hide-and-seek language, and returned to the toys. Here she did something quite deliberately seductive. She took the small electric light bulb with the face on it and put it to her mouth, eyeing me in a meaningful way, and then she held up her skirt and put it to her knickers. It was a kind of music-hall invitation. Along with this, she said she knew a naughty way of saying

Good King Wenceslas that her mother knows:

Gabrielle: Good King Wenceslas looked out on
the feast of Stephen.
A snowball hit him in the snout and
made it all uneven;
Brightly shone the moon that night
though the pain was cruel.
Then the doctor came in sight,
riding on a mule. . . .

In the course of this episode, which had some
generalized excitement in it, I had drawn the
dog, cooperating with her. It started as a copy
of the face on the bulb.

Gabrielle: I'll show you what I can draw. I
hardly do ears; it has long hair,
beautiful hair—look I've spilt over
on to the other paper, and on to the
table. It's a little scribble. . . .

I said here that it was as if she were drawing to
show me a dream, and some of the dream had
spilt over into waking life. It seemed that this
was what she wanted, for she now told me a
dream, and it felt as if this was perhaps what
she had come to tell me.

Gabrielle: I had a dream about you. I knocked
on the door of your house. I saw Dr.
Winnicott in the pool in his garden.
So I dived in. Daddy saw me in the
pool hugging and kissing Dr. Winnicott, so he dived in too. Then mum-

my dived in, then Susan, and [here
she enumerated the others of the
family including the four grand-
parents]. There were fishes and
everything. It was a dry wet water.
We all came out and walked in the
garden. Daddy landed on the beach.
It was a good dream.

I felt that she had now brought everything into
the transference and had in this way reorgan-
ized her entire life in terms of the experience of
a positive relationship to the subjective figure of
the analyst, and his inside.

> *Me:* The pool is here in this room, where
> everything has happened and where
> everything imaginatively can happen.

She said something about her hands being wet
because she was swimming.

Gabrielle: I'm going to draw what I can on the
lamp.

She was now quite happy and calm, and emptied out the small toys and bits of toys. She was
singing on the theme of "Together."

Gabrielle: What a mess on your floor!

I had to mend a hook. She talked a lot
while getting all the toys into use. Then she took
the father figure (about three inches long, very
realistic, made on a basis of pipe-cleaner) and
started to ill-treat it.

Gabrielle: I'm twisting his legs [etc.].

    Me: Ow! Ow! [as an interpretation of acceptance of the role assigned me].

Gabrielle: I'm twisting him more — yes — his arm now.

    Me: Ow!

Gabrielle: Now his neck!

    Me: Ow!

Gabrielle: Now there's nothing left — he's all twisted up. I am going to twist you some more. You cry more.

    Me: Ow! Ow! Ooooooo!

She was very pleased.

Gabrielle: Now there's nothing left. It's all twisted up and his leg came off, and now his head has come off, so you can't cry. I am throwing you right away. Nobody loves you.

    Me: So Susan can never have me.

Gabrielle: Everybody hates you.

Hate for hate (cf. previous session)

Here she took the similar figure of a boy and repeated the operation.

Gabrielle: I'm twisting the boy's legs [etc.].

In the middle of all this I said: "So the Winnicott you invented was all yours and he's now finished with, and no one else can ever have him."

She was urging me to cry more but I protested that I had no more cry left.

    Me: It's all gone away.

Gabrielle: Nobody will ever see you again. Are
you a doctor?

Me: Yes, I am a doctor and I could be
Susan's doctor, but the Winnicott
that you invented is finished forever.

Gabrielle: I made you.

She was handling the train (making train
noises).

Gabrielle: I want to get this off.

Me: It doesn't come off.

Indeed, she knew the tractor was joined to the
hay cart and could not be separated.

Gabrielle: Oh, dear, it doesn't come off.

She now said everything looked blue, and
she had taken the two Optrex baths and was
looking at the world through them. She asked
how they could be tied on over her eyes. This
gave her the feeling she was swimming or under
water. So we screwed our eyes up at each other.
I could hold the eye baths with my orbicularis
muscles, and after some practice she could hold
one.

Gabrielle: I'd like to take them home with me.

She then went on to talk about pottery frag-
ments found by the roadside in France, and
gave me a child's-eye view of archeology, finding what belonged to life a long time ago. She
now explored the tin of crayons and found or
rediscovered the Seccotine (an adhesive). This

was what she wanted, and she started on her last play (but she had other things to say—did I get a letter she sent me? And so on.).

She took a sheet of paper and put Seccotine in the middle and also as a square frame. She wanted to know how many more patients I would be seeing.

Me: You are the last before my holiday.
Gabrielle: I'm five, in a very little while.

She indicated that she had wanted to see me to get this treatment—Winnicott finished off while she was still four.

> *Me:* I'd like to get finished with you, too, so that I could be all the other Winnicotts and not have to be this special treatment Winnicott invented by you.

I could see that this thing she was doing with the Seccotine was a kind of gravestone or memorial of the Winnicott that had been destroyed and made dead. Following her intimation I took a piece of paper and drew a Gabrielle on it. Then I twisted its arms and legs and head, and I asked her if it hurt. She laughed, and she said: "No, it tickles!"

She did quite a lot of decorating round the Seccotine, including red. This was something to bring home. It would be nice for Susan.

Gabrielle: I must put a little more blue.

It got folded over and all the Seccotine was used

up, and I had to help her to make a hole so that string could be attached. It was now a kite.

Gabrielle: I must go to daddy and ask for the beautiful tiles, with the merry boy on them.

Leaving me to look after the kite, she went and fetched two antique tiles (merry boy) that her father had bought and that were wrapped up in paper as if as a present — presumably for mother. I took these out and admired them.
    She went on explaining to father.

Gabrielle: He is used up. Nobody wants to see Winnicott. Used all up. I tore it up. I have made this as a present for Susan. It's smelly, it's horrible — I've used the Seccotine right up. You'll have to buy some more, no more will come.

I added something here about pulling the plug to indicate the fecal significance of the destroyed male figures and the memorial tablet. This pleased her.

Gabrielle: It's all over my hands. I'm playing with horrible smelly sticky stuff. What is its name — oh yes, Seccotine, horrible name, horrible smell. We use Yoohoo, no smell you know. . . .

I could see that she had come to finish me off in all layers and in all senses, and I said so. She said: "Yes, to finish you off."

    Me: So if I came to visit your home, if I saw Susan, that would be a different Winnicott — not the one you invented who was all yours and who is now finished with.

Gabrielle: Now all the glue is used up — what shall we do? All the Winnicott all to pieces, what do we do when all is gone? Glad not to see Winnicott if he smells and is sticky like that. No one wants him. If you come to us, I'll say "The sticky man's coming." We'd run away.

This terminated.

Gabrielle: I like painting when I go to.... This is a nice paper. Is it time for me to go?

    Me: Yes, nearly.

Gabrielle: I must wash — I'll come back to see you. Color it red [the kite]!

I held it by its string while she washed. She came back for it and went off with her father, dragging and trying to fly her heavy, wet, sticky kite.

COMMENTS

    1. Blooming in age-appropriate maturation.

    2. Copes with separation and knows that reunion is available.

3. Exercising female seductiveness.

4. Summing up the analysis, having re-organized her life within a positive transference.

5. Thus hate can be safely felt and exercised since it would not destroy the good inter-analytic experience.

SIXTEENTH CONSULTATION
(October 28, 1966)

Gabrielle was now five years, two months old. This session was not like the previous visits. In fact it seemed more like a visit from a friend to a friend. After waiting with her father for five minutes, because they were early, the father went to the waiting room; she quickly took in the various changes in the room, and started to do what she obviously intended to do.

The hour that we spent together was divided into three parts, the first part being the most important. She asked for the steam roller. This is the cylindrical ruler. We had 25 minutes of the old game, which was played without great excitement, but with an intensity that belongs to games played at the age of five. She rolled the steam roller toward me, and when it hit my knees I died. When I was dead, she hid. By now we knew all the routes toward corners only too well. In the course of the game, she took up her positions one after another: I had to come alive, begin to remember that there was someone else whom I had forgotten, and then gradually search for her. Then at last I would find her. Sometimes it was she who died in the same way; then she searched for me. She went on until she was satisfied she had had enough of this. Then she entered into phase two.

While I sat in the little chair writing notes as in the old days, she sat on the floor with her back to me — "alone in my presence." She talked to the animals and the toys, and only occasionally made it clear to me that I was supposed to hear. At the beginning she took the lamb and said: "Where's the dog?" I found the envelope in which the remains of the dog live, and she told me all about the hole in it and explored the hole with her finger. She said that the dog was not too empty to stand, and she placed it standing beside the lamb. Then she began the taking out of the toys and emptied the bucket. For a time she was joining up a train, talking intelligibly, but to herself. Once she said: "Look at a long train I've made!" But it was not long because she was only remembering what it was like in the earlier sessions, not playing for the purpose of communication.

> *Me:* You are reminding yourself what the toys used to mean to you when you were a little Piggle instead of a big Gabrielle.
>
> *Gabrielle:* Let's play again.

And she carefully put a few toys she had taken out away again and tidied them up under the book shelf. While she was doing this she was handling a basket and other toys in a loving way and saying things such as: "There you are." In the course of this, her head touched my elbow. This was not something deliberate, nor did she shrink from it. It just happened. She put the dog away in its envelope and said goodbye. And she put the lamb next to the envelope. Then she said: "Now!" — meaning that we were going over into something different.

We got up, and at first it seemed as if we were to have more steam-roller play (hide and seek). What she did, however, was find a child's picture book. I sat down with her, and we turned over its leaves. She looked at the book with great care and seemed to enjoy the little bits of the story I was able to give. We then looked at another book which had plenty of pictures, but it was a bit too complicated, so we changed again and found a picture book with a story. I went over the story with her while she turned the pages. In the end, she chose to look through an animal book. Wherever possible she gave the names of the animals, and she was very happy and contented. I gave her the chance to talk to me about things; the word black came into one of the stories and I reminded her of the black mummy.

> *Me:* You are shy to tell me some of the things that you think.

She assented, but this seemed rather half-hearted.

Me: I know when you are really shy, and
that is when you want to tell me that
you love me.

She was very positive in her gesture of assent.

Now it was time to leave, and she was quite
ready to go and fetch her father. She had obviously enjoyed her visit, and I could find no
evidence whatever of her being disappointed as
if she had intended something and had left it
out. She seemed entirely natural when saying
goodbye, and I got the impression of a really
natural and psychiatrically normal girl of five
years.

AFTERWORD
By the Parents of the Piggle

Some readers may be interested in a few observations on the parents' experiences in this case, and may like to have some up-to-date facts about the child.

It has been of great value to the parents to be allowed to participate in a process of growth and reparation. This has prevented what can often be observed: the parents' feeling left out in the cold, and so perhaps prey to feelings of rivalry and competition with the therapist; or perhaps envy of either the therapist or the child, or alternatively in order to avoid such painful feelings, and to avoid the insidious obstructiveness that may result from them, parents may withdraw, stepping out of the field of forces of a live relationship with the child and just handing him over to a more skilled and knowledgeable authority.

Though the danger of an unprofessional mix-up may loom in some readers' minds, this seems to have been avoided by the tact, "feel," and long experience of the therapist, which appeared based on so great a knowledge that it could be as if forgotten again, and used in a free and spontaneous manner with a sureness of touch that could be relied upon.

Perhaps the parents might also be permitted to put in a word in any further discussion of the pros and cons of "on demand" treatment.

At the time we felt that we could not have accepted treatment on any other basis. Moreover, the consensus of feeling which grew up that the time for another session was ripe is remarkable, and we were indeed amazed on reading the script to realize how the patient took up the threads from the previous session as if no time had gone between, or as if she was now ready for the next step.

However, when within this framework treatment cannot take place when demanded (as between the eleventh and the twelfth sessions), there can be very violent repercussions, and, as it may seem in this case, very narrowly avoided inner disaster for the patient.

Readers may also want to know what the patient is like now, what are the long-term results of such a process of treatment.

Gabrielle is unself-conscious—a spontaneous girl, very much part of a group of contemporaries at school. She seems to have regained the poise that she had lost before she started treatment. Around the age of eight she had some learning difficulties (was bored at school and did not learn to read easily), but she is now very competent at her work, and always able to find something interesting in it. She is domestic rather than tomboyish in her inclinations. To be a teacher of biology seems at the moment to be what she wants to do. The growing of indoor plants is her chief hobby. It is her certainty of values, her inner independence of judgment, and also perhaps a way of being in touch with people on many wave-lengths, that make one wonder whether the leaven of some satisfying experience of being understood on a deep level may not be continuing to be still at work.

Later comments about the sessions were almost none — very rarely perhaps a chuckle about a memory, or some item of play. The sad news of Dr. Winnicott's death was brought by a casual visitor, and her immediate reactions were shrouded in the social situation. Dr. Winnicott had prepared her for the eventuality of his death in a most sensitive way, and she has since mentioned this session once or twice as it somehow fitted into place.

Dr. Winnicott used to take notes during the sessions, and Gabrielle thinks that he was writing his autobiography and that she somehow came to be involved in a small corner of it: "He used to write and I used to play."

When the publication of this material (which she has not yet seen) came to be discussed with her, she at first hesitated, but then thought that it may be of use to others — as indeed it is hoped it may be. She gave her consent.

1975